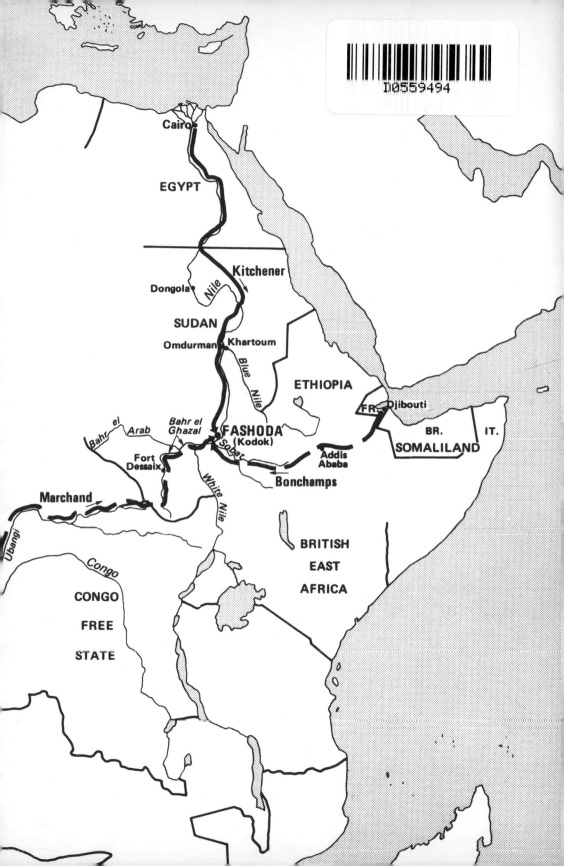

THE JOHNS HOPKINS UNIVERSITY STUDIES IN HISTORICAL AND POLITICAL SCIENCE

EIGHTY–EIGHTH SERIES (1970)

1. Fashoda Reconsidered: The Impact of Domestic Politics on French Policy in Africa, 1893–1898
By ROGER GLENN BROWN

FASHODA RECONSIDERED

FASHODA RECONSIDERED
The Impact of Domestic Politics on French Policy in Africa 1893-1898

By
ROGER GLENN BROWN

THE JOHNS HOPKINS PRESS
BALTIMORE AND LONDON

The Johns Hopkins Press, Baltimore, Maryland 21218
The Johns Hopkins Press Ltd., London
Library of Congress Catalog Card Number 70–94393

Standard Book Number 8018–1098–1

FOR LYNN AND CARA

CONTENTS

ACKNOWLEDGMENTS

I wish to express my sincere gratitude to:

Dr. Raymond J. Sontag, who first suggested that I investigate the relationship between the Dreyfus affair and Fashoda, and who gave me encouragement and direction while I was researching the topic;

Dr. Robert O. Paxton, whose guidance was particularly helpful during the early phases of my research;

Dr. Richard F. Kuisel, who carefully read the entire manuscript and made many valuable and thoughtful suggestions for improving it;

Dr. Edward M. Corbett, who greatly aided me with the translation of the French passages, and who made many helpful suggestions for improving portions of the manuscript;

M. François Berge, who not only made available to me the private papers of his grandfather, former French President Félix Faure, but also was kind enough to extend his personal hospitality to me and my wife in such a way that we felt more at home during our stay in Paris;

M. Georges Dethan, the archivist of the French Ministry of Foreign Affairs, who discussed with me the Papiers Hanotaux and the Papiers Delcassé at some length, and made available to me the uncatalogued and valuable Lettres de Delcassé;

Dr. Douglas Johnson, who wrote me a much appreciated letter encouraging me to continue to pursue my subject;

The NDEA authorities and the Committee on Research of the University of California, Berkeley, for making funds available which made trips to Paris and London for research purposes possible;

My wife Lynn, who gave me invaluable aid while researching and writing this study, who typed, retyped, and carefully proofread all drafts, and who, by her constant encouragement, inspired me to believe that my effort was worthwhile.

ABBREVIATIONS

AN: Archives Nationales

APP: Archives du Préfecture de Police

BCAF: *Bulletin du Comité de l'Afrique française*

BI: Bibliothèque de l'Institut

BN: Bibliothèque Nationale

CCO: Christ Church, Oxford

CDFF: Correspondance diplomatique de Félix Faure

DDF: *Documents diplomatiques français*

FO: Foreign Office, London

JAH: *Journal of African History*

MAE: Ministère des Affaires Etrangères

MC: Ministère des Colonies

MG: Ministère de la Guerre

MM: Ministère de la Marine

n. a. fr.:   nouvelle acquisition française

NPFF: Notes personnelles de Félix Faure

NS: Nouvelle Série

PRO: Public Record Office, London

INTRODUCTION

Domestic Politics and Foreign Policy:
The Problem and the Sources

In the autumn of 1898 the French Third Republic was convulsed simultaneously by two crises, one domestic, the other international. The first was the climax of the Dreyfus affair, which entered its most acute phase following the news of the *" faux Henry"* on 31 August 1898. The second was the climax of a decade of Franco-British imperialist rivalry for the Egyptian Sudan, which erupted into the Fashoda crisis in September and October 1898. Before the Dreyfus affair had run its course, France was on the verge of widespread civil violence; before the Fashoda crisis was resolved, France and Britain were closer to war than any European powers had been during the succession of pre-1914 confrontations over Africa. The conjuncture of these two crises focuses attention on the theme of this study: the impact of domestic politics on French policy in Africa during the period of the European partition of the continent.

II

The student of the impact of domestic politics on foreign policy finds few models upon which to base his investigation. In the past, historians have generally segregated their studies into rigidly defined categories, the one marked domestic, the other diplomatic. Diplomatic historians have directed their attention outward to shifting alliances and alignments between states, and have concentrated so exclusively on the role of statesmen in this process that they have created the impression that foreign policy was " crudely manufactured " in the foreign offices of Europe.[1] Domestic political historians have either ignored foreign affairs or, like Chastenet in his fine study of the Third Republic, have interrupted their narrative of internal events with separate chapters devoted to " *politique extérieure.*"[2]

1. A. J. P. Taylor, *The Struggle for Mastery in Europe* (Oxford, 1954), p. 569.
2. Jacques Chastenet, *Histoire de la Troisième République. III: La République triomphante 1893–1906* (Paris, 1955), chaps. 7 and 12.

1

Although this approach to international relations is far from extinct, it has come under increasing attack in recent years. Pierre Renouvin, for example, has long argued that the pure diplomatic approach should be abandoned. In its place he has suggested a "*plan de travail*" to guide future researchers in international relations who are interested in establishing the influence of domestic politics on foreign affairs.[3] Three broad areas of investigation have been outlined. The first deals with economic and financial influences, the second with the effects of demographic change, and the third with the impact of changes in the realm of "collective psychology." In his *Histoire des relations internationales*, Renouvin has shown how fruitful this approach can be.[4]

Renouvin's approach is best suited to middle-level investigations designed to demonstrate the impact of broad historical forces on policy over periods of three to four decades. My study has a more limited focus: it is a "micro-history" of a limited sequence of events, and therefore poses problems of a different order from those envisioned in Renouvin's *plan de travail*.[5]

Attention is focused on the problems of micro-history in Snyder, Bruck, and Spain's *Foreign Policy Decision-Making: An Approach to the Study of International Politics*.[6] The goal of this theoretical monograph is to construct a frame of reference for the study of international relations which poses researchable problems that can be answered by a series of case studies. Although at times the

3. Pierre Renouvin, "L'Histoire contemporaine des relations internationales: orientation de recherches," *Revue historique*, CCXI (1954), 233–55. The central themes of this pioneering essay have been elaborated on in a recent book: Renouvin and Jean-Baptiste Duroselle, *Introduction à l'histoire des relations internationales* (Paris, 1964).

4. Renouvin, *Histoire des relations internationales. VI: Le XIXe siècle* (Paris, 1955).

5. Fernand Braudel has distinguished three levels of historical investigation. At the deepest level is "structural" history, which examines long periods of time and seeks to characterize entire epochs. Middle-level investigations of shorter periods of time attempt to explain the conjuncture between social, economic, and political change in time. Finally, at the top "layer" is "micro-history," which is concerned with events in a relatively short span of time and with the conscious actions and decisions of men. See Braudel, "Histoire et sociologie," in *Traité de sociologie*, ed. Georges Gurvitch, 2nd ed. (Paris, 1962), I, 82–97. Cited by Maurice Duverger, *An Introduction to the Social Sciences with Special Reference to their Methods* (New York, 1961), pp. 31–33.

6. Richard C. Snyder, H. W. Bruck, and Burton Sapin, eds., *Foreign Policy Decision-Making: An Approach to the Study of International Politics* (New York, 1962), pp. 14–186.

study may seem too abstract for the working historian, it is far more adaptable to historical studies than most of the systems conceived by contemporary social scientists.[7] My monograph has not abandoned the classic tools of the historian, but it has profited from many of the definitions and concepts developed by decision-making analysis.

Snyder and his colleagues define international politics as " processes of state interaction at the governmental level," and stress the importance of " official decision-makers," that is, those " acting in the name of the state." The " prime analytical objective " of this theory is the " re-creation of the ' world ' of the decision-makers as they view it." [8]

To accomplish this objective, decision-making analysis introduces the concept of setting, " an analytical term which reminds us that the decision-makers act upon and respond to conditions and factors which exist outside themselves and the governmental organization of which they are a part. . . . Setting is really a set of categories of potentially relevant factors and conditions which may affect the actions of any state." [9] There are two aspects to setting: external and internal. External setting consists of " factors and conditions beyond the territorial boundaries of the state "; internal setting comprises factors and conditions within the state.[10] Thus, the world of the decision-maker is a response, often simultaneous, to both external and internal demands.[11]

The diplomatic historian has always attempted to re-create the world of the diplomatist and to show how this world affected his decisions. As a result of the documentation which he used, however, his efforts have mainly been directed toward reconstruction of the external setting of the decision-making situation.[12] " Our sources," writes A. J. P. Taylor, " are primarily the records which foreign offices keep of their dealings with each other; and the

7. Neither Thomas Schelling, *The Strategy of Conflict* (Cambridge, Mass., 1960), nor Morton Kaplan, *System and Process in International Politics* (New York, 1957), proved helpful except in the most general way.

8. Snyder *et al.*, *Foreign Policy*, p. 66.

9. *Ibid.*, p. 67.

10. *Ibid.*, p. 65.

11. For a discussion of the problem of simultaneity, see Snyder *et al.*, *Foreign Policy*, p. 59.

12. Major exceptions to this generalization are the pioneering studies by Arno J. Mayer, *Wilson vs. Lenin: Political Origins of the New Diplomacy, 1917–1918* (Cleveland, 1964), and *Politics and Diplomacy of Peacemaking, Containment and Counterrevolution at Versailles, 1918–1919* (New York, 1967).

writer who bases himself solely on the archives is likely to claim scholarly virtue." [13]

From the diplomatic archives it is possible to construct the external setting of decision-making and, to some extent, the diplomatic response to the domestic setting. But, unless these documents are used with imagination, studies of "scholarly virtue" which rely solely on them often deserve G. N. Young's epithet: "What A said to B, and B said to C; that's diplomatic history."

Although it does not ignore what A said to B, decision-making analysis does place their conversation in a broader context, and this is a key contribution. Decision-making theorists have not solved all of the problems for the student of domestic and international politics, but they have pointed the way toward new questions and new sources of documentation beyond the records of the foreign office.

III

Part I of my study, "Domestic Politics and the Formulation of Foreign Policy," deals with the period between 1893 and 1898, the formulatory phase of the decision-making process which defined French policy toward the Upper Nile. During this period the French government launched a series of expeditions toward the Upper Nile basin near the ancient fort of Fashoda in the Egyptian Sudan. The last of these succeeded, and its success produced the Fashoda confrontation, a major international crisis which seriously affected France's general position in European politics and strained Franco-British relations to the breaking point. The Upper Nile project, therefore, represented an extremely serious national undertaking, and was the result of a succession of major foreign policy decisions.

Decisions of this order of importance were the responsibility of the French Minister of Foreign Affairs, the permanent officials of the Foreign Ministry at the Quai d'Orsay, and the diplomatic corps. Their decisions were a response to both external and internal factors. A number of studies have reconstructed the external setting of the Upper Nile policy decisions; [14] no investigator has dealt systematically with those factors in the internal setting which influenced Foreign Ministry decision-makers.

13. Taylor, *Struggle for Mastery*, p. 569.
14. The best accounts are Renouvin, "Les origines de l'expédition de Fachoda," *Revue historique*, CC (1948), 180–97, and G. N. Sanderson, *England, Europe and the Upper Nile 1882–1890* (Edinburgh, 1965), pp. 140–290. Sanderson's book will be cited below with only the author's name and page numbers.

One important factor was interdepartmental politics. Today, foreign policy decisions are the result of the interplay of a number of governmental groups. Rather than a homogeneous decision-making group, a modern government is a complex set of groups which in theory work together harmoniously but in practice are often in conflict with one another.[15] This was also true in the nineteenth century, though few historians have explored the problem. In addition to the Ministry of Foreign Affairs, the Ministries of War, Marine, and Colonies were involved in defining French relations toward the outside world.

The Ministry of Colonies played a central role in the formulation of Upper Nile policy. G. N. Sanderson underlined this point in his study, *England, Europe and the Upper Nile,* but he was unable to trace the problem further because of a gap in documentation. " All papers relating to the incubation of the Marchand Mission," lamented Sanderson, " were removed, in the course of 1938 and in June 1939, from the Colonial Ministry files by the then Minister, Georges Mandel; and they have not been recovered." [16] Afrique III, 32a, the crucial dossier which Mandel examined in 1939, was rediscovered in April 1963 and is now available at the Colonial Ministry's archives.[17] The records of the colonial army on the Marchand mission are also accessible to scholars. This new evidence clearly demonstrates the importance of interdepartmental politics in the 1890's.

In addition, the new material at the Ministry of Colonies makes possible a clarification of the role of the nonparliamentary career professional in the formulation of policy. It has long been assumed that ministerial instability increased the importance of this group in the ministries of the Third Republic. The " initiative in policy formulation," wrote Frederick L. Schuman, " may actually come from the permanent bureaucrats rather than from the responsible minister." [18] It is now possible to test this hypothesis.

15. Roger Hilsman, *To Move a Nation* (New York, 1967), gives a description of the present-day situation in the United States.

16. Sanderson, p. 272.

17. Marchand's original project proposal of 11 September 1895, a document for which archivists and historians have been searching since the compilation of volume XIV of the *Documents diplomatiques français* in 1949, is included in Afrique III, 32a. See *Documents diplomatiques français (DDF),* XIV, Foreword, ix.

18. Frederick L. Schuman, *War and Diplomacy in the Third French Republic* (Chicago, 1931), p. 30.

Another important element of the internal setting was pressure group politics. The importance of pressure groups in the formulation of foreign policy is generally recognized, but, as Jean Meynaud has observed, our knowledge is still limited to conjecture based on a very few concrete examples.[19] The scarcity of detailed case studies in this field is a result of the near absence of significant documentary sources. When Henri Brunschwig conducted his pioneering study on the important Comité de l'Afrique française, he relied almost solely on the published *Bulletin* of the group.[20] Although the *Bulletin* is an important source, it reveals only the public image of the group and how the Comité sought to influence public opinion. More important for our purposes are other " *styles d'action*," such as the access-gaining techniques employed by the Comité to influence the decision-making process more directly.[21]

A record of the Comité's behind-the-scenes tactics is revealed in an unpublished collection of documents, the Fonds Auguste Terrier, now deposited at the Bibliothèque de l'Institut. The 132 dossiers collected here are the work of Auguste Terrier, who was a secretary-general of the Comité and the brother-in-law of Hippolyte Percher, one of the Comité's founders. Terrier, who was a careful archivist, performed an invaluable service for future historians when he systematically collected and organized the records of one of the most successful pressure groups in the history of the Third Republic.[22] I have exploited all of the policy statements and correspondence related to the Upper Nile project in an effort to go beyond simple conjecture and to demonstrate in a concrete case how pressure-group politics influenced foreign policy.

A number of case studies have dealt with the influence of parliamentary politics on foreign affairs.[23] The primary conclusions of

19. Jean Meynaud, *Nouvelles études sur les groupes de pression* (Paris, 1962), p. 390.

20. Henri Brunschwig, " Le Parti colonial français," *Revue française d'histoire d'outremer*, XLVI (1959), 49–93, later incorporated into *Mythes et réalités de l'impérialisme colonial français, 1871–1914* (Paris, 1960).

21. See Meynaud, *Nouvelles études*, especially chaps. 4 and 5.

22. Terrier's general concern with the preservation of historical documents is revealed by one of his few published articles: " Pour sauver nos archives d'Afrique," *Bulletin du Comité de l'Afrique française (BCAF)*, XXIII (August 1913), 293–95.

23. Schuman, *War and Diplomacy*, pp. 21–26, and Joseph Barthélemy, *Démocratie et politique étrangère* (Paris, 1919), both give general treatments. Case studies include Bertha Leaman, " The Influence of Domestic Policy on Foreign Affairs in France, 1898-1905," *Journal of Modern History*, XIV (1942), 449–79; and John C. Cairns, " Politics and Foreign Policy: The French Parliament, 1911–1914," *Canadian History Review*, XXXIV (1953), 245–76.

these investigations are that (1) the elected representatives of France were on the whole uninterested in external affairs and (2) the parliament exercised almost no control over foreign policy makers. Although my study does not dispute these views, it does show that a small parliamentary group took a sustained interest in foreign affairs, and that this vocal minority could, and did, influence policy without controlling it.

Cabinet politics also influenced French foreign policy. Although under the Third Republic the cabinet was collectively responsible for the formulation of external as well as internal policy, most ministers concentrated their attention on domestic politics, and the views of the Minister of Foreign Affairs were usually accepted in the area of his competence.[24] On occasion, however, the Minister of Foreign Affairs was overruled by his colleagues for reasons which were probably linked to domestic rather than international considerations. It was on one of these occasions that the Dreyfus case seems to have first influenced the course of events which eventually led to the Fashoda crisis.

Certain general themes of this study should now be clear. Of a variety of internal factors which could be investigated, I have concentrated on the following problems: (1) interdepartmental politics, (2) the effects of ministerial instability, (3) pressure group politics, (4) parliamentary politics, and (5) cabinet politics. These internal factors decisively influenced French Upper Nile policy in the period between 1893 and 1898, and continued to trouble decision-makers during the Fashoda crisis itself. But in addition to these general factors, the Fashoda crisis was complicated by a phenomenon which came to dominate almost all French political life in 1898—the Dreyfus affair.

IV

Part II of my study, "Domestic Crisis and the Conduct of Foreign Policy," is a reconstruction of events in the months immediately prior to and during the Dreyfus-Fashoda crisis, January–November 1898. Prior to January 1898, the Dreyfus affair was not a major issue in French politics. Until that time the brother of Alfred Dreyfus, Mathieu, and the small group of men around him had endeavored to have the case revised. They had achieved

24. Schuman, *War and Diplomacy*, pp. 20–21.

only limited success, however, when Emile Zola published his
" J'accuse " in *L'Aurore* in January 1898. This event " politicized "
the affair on both the domestic and international planes by initi-
ating currents of revisionist and antirevisionist sentiment.[25] By
the summer of 1898, however, the revisionist cause was subsiding
into a sea of apathy.

The entire situation was drastically altered by the announcement
on 31 August that Colonel Henry, head of the army's Section de
Statistique, the group in charge of intelligence and counter-
intelligence, had been arrested for forging a document to prove
the guilt of Dreyfus. The storm produced by the *faux Henry* was
much more serious than the Zola affair had ever been. Pro- and
anti-Dreyfus groups staged a series of political demonstrations,
and there were many bloody conflicts between these two opposing
armies. The situation was further complicated by a vast, almost
general, strike of the Parisian working class, to which the government responded by garrisoning the streets of Paris with troops
from the provinces. The Dreyfusards raised the specter of a
military coup d'état; the anti-Dreyfusards were frightened by the
prospect of imminent revolution. The Dreyfus affair, therefore,
was transformed in the fall of 1898 into a major domestic crisis.

Many studies have observed that the most dramatic political
consequences of the affair came after 31 August 1898. Langer
writes that " the autumn and winter of 1898–1899 was perhaps
the most critical period in the whole domestic history of the Third
Republic prior to the World War," and " the Dreyfus case
reached the climactic phase and threatened to assume the character of a civil war . . ." [26] Chapman concludes: " There was thus
enough explosive opinion in Paris . . . to make nervous people
foresee some outbreak, some new ' Grande Peur,' a prelude, if not
to another 1789, at least to riots." [27] Yet as serious as the Dreyfus
crisis was assessed to be, there still exists no monograph which
deals systematically with the events of the fall and winter of
1898. Volume IV of Reinach's classic *Histoire de l'affaire Dreyfus*,
because of its encyclopedic scope and the writer's personal experi-

25. The international response to Zola's letter is heavily documented: Ministère
des Affaires Etrangères (MAE), Allemagne: Nouvelle série (NS) 53, Politique
étrangère, Affaire Dreyfus.

26. William L. Langer, *The Diplomacy of Imperialism*, 2nd ed. (New York,
1951), p. 554.

27. Guy Chapman, *The Dreyfus Case: A Reassessment* (London, 1955), p. 235.

ence of events, still remains the best introduction to this period
after over sixty years of scholarship. Although I have not attempted to produce the much-needed monograph on the immediate political consequences of the Dreyfus affair, I have sought
new sources, the most important of which are in the archives of
the Prefecture of Police, Department of the Seine. These new
sources throw light on the complex events which became so closely
linked with the Fashoda crisis.

The use of the archives of the Prefecture raises the question
of how important Parisian politics were in the shaping of foreign
policy. The French foreign policy establishment, by the very fact
of its geographical location, was subject to the political atmosphere
of Paris. In 1898 the newspapers which Delcassé's press assistant
clipped and placed on the Minister's desk were all Parisian
dailies.[28] There is no evidence that Delcassé ever consulted his
constituents in Ariège before making policy decisions.[29] Finally,
it is certain that when non-French diplomatic observers sought to
define the possible impact of domestic politics on French foreign
policy, their observations were drawn primarily from events within
Paris. The Dreyfus crisis as it was seen from the vantage point
of the British embassy on rue du Faubourg Sainte Honoré was
above all a Parisian crisis.

After January 1898 European diplomats stationed in France
began to reflect on the possible international consequences of the
growing domestic unrest in France. In September and October the
question assumed momentous proportions for the British diplomatic establishment in Paris. It was the difficult task of Sir
Edmund Monson, the British ambassador, and his military attaché,
Colonel Douglas Dawson, to carefully observe the changing situation in France, and to forecast how the Dreyfus crisis would
affect French attitudes and actions toward Great Britain during
the course of the Fashoda crisis. In the end the British response
to internal developments in France probably had a decisive influence on the outcome of the Fashoda crisis.

This is not at all evident after an investigation of the published
diplomatic documents on the crisis. Volume I of the *British
Documents on the Origins of the War, 1898–1914* includes only
two of Monson's reports that mention the domestic crisis. This

28. MAE, Papiers Delcassé, carton 16: Dossier de presse (1898-1899).
29. *Ibid.*, carton 14: Elections législatives (Ariège) 1895-1915.

does not demonstrate that Monson or decision-makers in London were indifferent to the impact of domestic politics on foreign affairs, but rather that the editors of the collection, G. P. Gooch and H. W. V. Temperley, belonged to the old school of diplomatic history and were unconcerned with domestic problems. From the point of view of diplomatic history, the Fashoda crisis was important only as a turning point in the history of Franco-British relations, and this explains why certain documents were selected for publication and others ignored.[30] The glaring gaps in the published documents have been supplemented by Foreign Office correspondence at the Public Record Office, and by the Salisbury Papers at Christ Church, Oxford.

The published collection of French diplomatic documents, though more complete than its British counterpart, contains little information on the question of how the French Minister of Foreign Affairs, Théophile Delcassé, responded to the conjuncture of the Dreyfus and Fashoda crises.[31] This is not the result of the attitudes of the editors of the collection, however;[32] rather it is due to the attitude of the Foreign Minister himself.

In the early 1890's, after Delcassé's first tenure as Undersecretary of State for Colonies, a band of his political opponents gained access to government records and, in an effort to discredit him, publicized several of Delcassé's confidential reports.[33] This experience perhaps explains the behavior of Delcassé after he became Minister of Foreign Affairs in the summer of 1898. His communications with his ambassadors were always guarded and seldom contained any extended explanations of the reasoning behind his policy decisions. He developed the habit of giving verbal orders, and for the most part relied on his excellent memory instead of making rough drafts of his conversations with other European diplomats.[34] Robert de Billy, a member of the Foreign

---

30. Taylor, *From Napoleon to Stalin: Comments on European History* (London, 1950), pp. 93–97.

31. *DDF*, XIV, Foreword, ix.

32. In fact, the editors stress the importance of the Dreyfus affair.

33. Charles W. Porter, *The Career of Théophile Delcassé* (Philadelphia, 1936), p. 92.

34. MAE, Papiers Delcassé, Introduction, pp. 5–6; Lettres de Delcassé, Mme. Noguès' Preface, p. iii. According to his daughter, Delcassé could recite Virgil at length, and after two readings could commit a page of verse to memory. While Minister of Foreign Affairs he memorized the names and career backgrounds of all major French representatives abroad.

Minister's *cabinet*, later observed: " Only Proust could be as silent [as Delcassé] on what touched him most deeply." [35]

Delcassé's systematic commitment to silence and his personal " weeding " of the Marchand-Fashoda files in 1904 account for the vacuum at the center of the published *Documents diplomatiques français*.[36] This lacuna of source material on the cryptic Foreign Minister was long lamented by French scholars, but the hope remained that it would be filled when Delcassé's private papers were made available.[37] Unfortunately, the Papiers Delcassé, which are now open to scholars, are not as significant a contribution as their sheer mass—twenty-five bulky cartons—might lead an archivist or historian to suspect. They have one serious fault: the thousands of documents in the collection include almost no letters or notes written by Delcassé himself. The Papiers Delcassé, therefore, do not represent the personal papers of the Foreign Minister but rather the papers which he accumulated over the long span of his political career.

In only one collection of documents are Delcassé's inner thoughts on domestic and international politics made explicit. When his daughter, the late Madame Noguès, delivered the Papiers Delcassé to the archives of the Ministry of Foreign Affairs, she withheld a dossier of her father's letters because they contained many statements of a purely family nature which she did not wish to have made public. These letters were deposited at a later date, however, and were edited in order to protect the family's privacy. They are bound in a small volume entitled Lettres de Delcassé, à sa femme, à sa fille, à quelques amis, 1885–1923. The volume, which was not catalogued, was made available to me through the courtesy of Monsieur Georges Dethan, head of the Foreign Ministry's archives.

The most interesting of these letters were sent by Delcassé to his wife while she was away from Paris on vacation. They are especially complete for the period of August–October 1898. Delcassé wrote them with only one view in mind—to describe to his wife his trials and hopes during his first months in office as Foreign Minister. The letters provide us with a rare insight into the

35. MAE, Lettres de Delcassé, Mme. Noguès' Preface, p. v.
36. *DDF*, XIV, Foreword, ix.
37. Renouvin, *La Politique extérieure de Théophile Delcassé* (*1898–1905*) (Paris: Centre de Documentation Universitaire, 1954), p. 1.

thinking of the key decision-maker at the French Ministry of Foreign Affairs as he sought to deal simultaneously with the Dreyfus and Fashoda affairs.[38]

This ministry was not the only French decision-making center involved in the crisis. The Ministry of Colonies was, of course, concerned and active before and after Delcassé initiated the diplomatic dialogue with Britain. The Ministry of War played an important role because it controlled the collection of political and military intelligence relating to the situation.[39] And when Fashoda advanced to an extremely critical stage toward the end of October and tension mounted to the very threshold of open violence, the Ministry of Marine became intimately involved.

Because Fashoda was a confrontation with Great Britain rather than with Germany, it was, in its military dimension, pre-eminently a naval crisis. Although the naval archives of Great Britain have been used brilliantly by Marder in a chapter entitled " Fashoda: A Lesson in Sea Power," no study has been published which exploits the French naval archives.[40] This is so even though J. H. Hexter has written: " If ever three human activities were inextricably bound together, scarcely intelligible save when conjoined, they are diplomacy, land warfare, and naval action." [41] On the basis of the extensive documents preserved in the naval archives, my study has reconstructed the relationship between diplomacy and naval power in the Fashoda crisis.

V

" The story of the crisis of the autumn of 1898," wrote a British newspaperman at the time, " is one of the cases in which history will have to be written more than once." [42] In the many rewritings

38. Some of the Lettres de Delcassé are cited by A. Maurois, *King Edward and His Times* (London, 1933). See also Christopher Andrew, *Théophile Delcassé and the Making of the Entente Cordiale* (New York, 1968), the most recent and best study on Delcassé. Andrew, who was allowed access to these letters before they were deposited at the Quai d'Orsay, was primarily concerned with the traditional question of Fashoda's place in the history of Franco-British relations, and did not systematically investigate the impact of the Dreyfus affair on the course of events.

39. The Section de Statistique of the French General Staff controlled both the overt and covert collection of political and military information, and the documents to 1900 are now available. See above, n. 35 for a further discussion of this problem.

40. A. J. Marder, *The Anatomy of British Sea Power: A History of British Naval Policy in the Pre-Dreadnought Era, 1880–1905* (New York, 1940).

41. J. H. Hexter, *Reappraisals in History* (New York, 1961), p. 195.

42. Thomas Barclay, *Thirty Years: Anglo-French Reminiscences* (London, 1914), p. 148.

of these events which have appeared since Thomas Barclay made this observation a half-century ago, no study has dealt systematically with the role played by domestic politics in general, and the Dreyfus affair in particular, in the origin, course, and outcome of the Fashoda crisis. Moreover, the new sources of information discussed in this introduction have never been exploited with the question of the impact of domestic politics in mind. Thus, a reconsideration of these events appears to be necessary.

Fashoda has continued to provoke the historical imagination over the last half-century largely because of its unique place as the most serious crisis during the partition of Africa. In his pioneering essay, "Towards a History of the Partition of Africa," John D. Hargreaves has argued that "Africanists should curb any tendency to disdain the contributions of diplomatic historians [because] often detailed knowledge of the European [diplomatic] situation is the key to the policies adopted by the Powers in Africa." [43] A basic premise of my study is that detailed knowledge of the domestic political situation is also central to any explanation of European policies in Africa, and that only by going beyond pure diplomatic history to the domestic sources of policy will European decisions regarding Africa become more intelligible.

In his *Reappraisals in History* J. H. Hexter lamented that historians had "split the past into a series of tunnels . . . practically self-contained at every point and sealed off from contact with or contamination by anything that was going on in any of the other tunnels." [44] The "tunnel method of history" artificially separated domestic from diplomatic and diplomatic from military history; it therefore failed to penetrate to what has recently been called the "central mystery" of international relations—the "nexus between the domestic and external aspects of state affairs." [45] The purpose of this monograph, then, is not only to reconsider a fascinating past event in the light of new evidence, but also to break down the barriers between domestic, diplomatic, and military history, and thereby illuminate in some small measure the central mystery of international relations.

43. John D. Hargreaves, "Towards a History of the Partition of Africa," *Journal of African History* (*JAH*), I (1960), 99.

44. Hexter, *Reappraisals*, p. 195.

45. David Vital, "On Approaches to the Study of International Relations," *World Politics*, XIX (1967), 561.

PART I

DOMESTIC POLITICS AND THE FORMULATION OF FOREIGN POLICY

CHAPTER I

DOMESTIC POLITICS AND FRENCH POLICY TOWARD THE UPPER NILE, 1893–95

During the Third Republic there existed two general currents of opinion on the proper orientation of French foreign policy, one continentalist, the other colonialist.[1] For the continentalists the Franco-German War decided the issue: the most serious problem facing France was in Europe; France was isolated diplomatically and was under the constant threat of a united and powerful Germany. The continentalists decided, therefore, that all French energies and resources should be devoted to meeting the German challenge. To divert men and resources to colonial expansion, they concluded, would weaken rather than strengthen France. The colonialists countered this by arguing that France was a world power as well as a European power; that French influence in world politics was a function of the size of the empire; and that the effort that went into expansionist projects would significantly strengthen the European position of France in the long run. In theory, therefore, it was possible to reconcile the two positions advocated by the colonialists and the continentalists; in practice there was an acute tension between the two currents of opinion.

The tension between the continentalists and the colonialists found its institutional expression in interdepartmental rivalry between the Ministry of Foreign Affairs and the governmental body which was charged with colonial affairs.[2] Throughout the

1. Renouvin, *La Politique extérieure de la Troisième République de 1871 à 1904* (Paris: Centre de Documentation Universitaire, 1953), pp. 43–50.
2. See Joannes Tramond and André Reussner, *Eléments d'histoire maritime et coloniale contemporaine (1815–1914)* (Paris, 1924). For a case study see C. W. Newbury, "The Development of French Policy on the Lower and Upper Niger, 1880–1898," *Journal of Modern History*, XXXI (1959), 16–26. "As in the case of other colonial questions," wrote Newbury, "the French foreign office did not always see eye-to-eye with the ministry for the navy or the colonial department attached to the ministry."

nineteenth century, colonial affairs were seldom directly under the control of the Ministry of Foreign Affairs. For the first two-thirds of the century colonial questions had been dealt with at the Ministry of Marine, and this department was the prime mover in the gradual rebuilding of the French overseas empire which had been almost completely destroyed during the Napoleonic wars.[3] The Third Republic created an Undersecretariat of State for Colonies which was attached at various times to the Ministry of Foreign Affairs, the Ministry of Commerce, and the Ministry of Marine. In the late 1880's and early 1890's colonialists began to demand the creation of an independent ministry to deal with colonial affairs, and in 1894 the Undersecretariat for Colonies was raised to the status of a full ministerial post.[4] The Undersecretariat for Colonies, later the Ministry of Colonies, was the governmental center of the colonialist tendency in foreign affairs. The Ministry of Foreign Affairs was the official locus of the continentalist tendency in foreign affairs. This made for tension between the two departments.[5]

Until the 1880's, the period when colonial questions were dealt with at the Ministry of Marine, French expansion was concentrated largely in the Far East. During this period France acquired numerous Pacific island bases and the nucleus of the Indochinese empire.[6] In the 1880's French expansion in the Far East continued, but at the same time the exploits of the French explorer Savorgnan

3. For the first half of the nineteenth century this thesis is presented in two excellent studies by Christian Schéfer: " La Politique coloniale de la première restauration: le dessein," *Annales des sciences politiques,* XVI (1901), 299-320, and *La Politique coloniale de la monarchie de juillet* (Paris, 1928). For the Second Empire this theme emerges from an excellent collection of documents: Georges Taboulet, *Le Geste française en indochine* (Paris, 1955). The Ministry of Marine remained an influential advocate of expansion during the first two decades of the Third Republic: see Thomas F. Power, *Jules Ferry and the Renaissance of French Imperialism* (New York, 1954), pp. 158–60; and C. W. Newbury and A. S. Kanya-Forstner, " French Policy and the Origins of the Scramble for West Africa," *JAH,* X (1969), 253–76.

4. See the painstaking account of this governmental change in François Berge, " Le Sous-Secrétariat et les Sous-Secrétaires d'Etat aux Colonies: histoire de l'émancipation de l'administration coloniales," *Revue française d'histoire d'outremer,* XLVII (1960), 301–86.

5. This is not to say that there was no interest in colonial expansion at the Quai d'Orsay, but rather that the primary orientation of the majority of personnel there in the 1890's, including the Foreign Ministers, was continentalist.

6. See John Frank Cady, *The Roots of French Imperialism in Eastern Asia* (New York, 1954), for an excellent account.

de Brazza captured the imagination of a segment of the colonial movement, and attention increasingly focused on Africa rather than Asia.[7] The emergent Ministry of Colonies took the lead in the shift from an Asian to an African emphasis, and while the Quai d'Orsay concentrated on the diplomacy of the Franco-Russian entente, the colonial department devoted most of its energies to the scramble for African colonies. On African questions, therefore, the Ministry of Foreign Affairs had to deal with an increasingly independent bureaucratic group which was anxious to assert its influence and to play a central role in the definition of policy.

II

Colonial pressure groups recognized and exploited the interdepartmental rivalry between the Ministries of Colonies and of Foreign Affairs. In fact, the most important African colonial pressure group and the purest embodiment of the colonialist tendency in France, the Comité de l'Afrique française, was founded in 1890 as a protest against official Foreign Ministry policy toward Africa. It had the support of the then Undersecretary of State for Colonies, Eugène Étienne.[8]

One of the principal founders of the French Comité was Hippolyte Percher, a Parisian journalist who went by the name of Harry Alis.[9] In the summer of 1890 Alis corresponded with Prince d'Arenberg, a French deputy and one of the largest landowners in France; the two men were soon agreed that unless there was immediate and energetic action France would be excluded from the entire African continent.[10] Prince d'Arenberg told Alis that he was prepared to support French expansion in Africa " *dans*

7. Jean Stengers, " L'Impérialisme colonial de la fin du XIXe siècle: mythe ou réalité," *JAH*, III (1962), 474–77.

8. Brunschwig, *Mythes et réalités*, p. 211. Andrew, *Théophile Delcassé*, correctly points out that the Comité was not founded in protest against the Anglo-French convention of August 1890, but there can be no doubt that its founders were opposed to official French policy as embodied in the convention, p. 34. See below, pp. 22–23.

9. In his funeral oration for Percher in 1895 Prince d'Arenberg called him the " *véritable organisateur*" of the Comité de l'Afrique française, *Le Temps*, 6 March 1895. In the Fonds Terrier, Percher is referred to as the " *fondateur du Comité*," Bibliothèque de l'Institut (BI), Fonds Terrier, 5891–92: Correspondance de Hippolyte Percher dit Harry Alis (1857–1895). Sanderson, therefore, is mistaken when he writes that Eugène Etienne " founded" the Comité in November 1890 (p. 119).

10. BI, Fonds Terrier, 5891, no. 3: Prince d'Arenberg to Alis, 31 July 1890.

la limite de mes forces," and that it was necessary to constitute a *" Comité d'études "* to deal with African questions.[11] Out of this exchange of letters grew the Comité de l'Afrique française. In exchange for his financial support and unrelenting efforts on behalf of the expansionist cause, Prince d'Arenberg was made president of the new group. Alis became its secretary-general.[12]

The first *Bulletin du Comité de l'Afrique française* appeared in 1891. At that time the Comité had twenty-nine members who defined themselves as " a certain number of persons animated by patriotic zeal " deeming it " necessary to put their African activities on a permanent basis." At a meeting on 19 November 1890 the members of the Comité agreed on the following statement: " We are witnessing something that has never before been seen in history: the veritable partition of an unknown continent by certain European countries. In this partition, France is entitled to the largest share . . ." [13] It was the goal of the Comité to insure that France did in fact obtain " the largest share " of the African continent. The chosen instruments for attaining this goal were propaganda in France and the launching of missions to Africa to extend French influence into uncharted areas.

In November 1891 Alis took account of the first year of the Comité's activities in a report to Prince d'Arenberg. Although some progress had been made in the organization and extension of the group's influence in France, the secretary-general concluded that the " government seems to view the work of the Comité with indifference at the present time." In order to deal with this governmental indifference it was decided to organize those deputies who were sympathetic to the goals of the Comité.[14] In July 1892 the *Bulletin* announced that " a colonial group has recently been formed in the Chamber, consisting of a large number of deputies belonging to different political tendencies but united by a desire to ensure France's strength and greatness in colonial and foreign spheres." [15] The chairman of the colonial group was Eugène

11. *Ibid.*, no. 4: Prince d'Arenberg to Alis, 12 September 1890.

12. Alis was killed in a duel in March 1895. He was eventually succeeded as secretary-general by his brother-in-law, Auguste Terrier.

13. *BCAF*, I (January 1891), 1–2.

14. BI, Fonds Terrier, 5891, no. 18: " Rapport adressé par le secrétaire général à Monsieur le Prince d'Arenberg, président du Comité de l'Afrique française," 15 November 1891.

15. *BCAF*, II (July 1892), 16.

Etienne, one of the early supporters of the Comité; Prince d'Arenberg was a vice-chairman.

There were only ninety-one members on the colonial group, but with the help of the Comité they exercised an influence in colonial matters far out of proportion to their number. This was primarily because the group was " alone among all political groups in France at the close of the nineteenth century in having a serious interest in foreign affairs." [16] They played an important role in gaining the Chamber's approval for the creation of an independent Ministry of Colonies. Whenever the Comité wished pressure to be exerted in the formulation of foreign policy, it could count on a member of the group like Deloncle or Flourens to make rancorous demands from the floor of the Chamber.[17]

The degree to which the threat of such demands could influence the government became apparent as early as December 1892. After discussing French politics with a Belgian diplomat who had recently returned from Paris, the British ambassador in Brussels wrote:

> They [all the officials with whom the Belgian had dealt] made no scruple in telling him that these details of the frontier line were of no earthly importance to France; that the territory they already had was more than sufficient; and that their only reason for standing out for more was the fear of being denounced in the Chamber for abandoning territory to which France may have a legitimate claim. They had said at this moment that the most insignificant of deputies might cover himself with glory by jumping up and impugning the convention as a sacrifice of French rights, a piece of rodomontade which would be rewarded by a crushing vote of censure on the Government.[18]

Until the first decade of the twentieth century, " the Chamber lacked an effective body of anti-Colonialist sentiment able to challenge the influence of the *groupe colonial.*" [19]

16. Andrew, *Théophile Delcassé*, p. 53. For a more detailed discussion of the colonial group, see Brunschwig, " Le Parti colonial," pp. 49–93.

17. See below, p. 51.

18. Public Record Office, London (PRO), Foreign Office (FO)10/595, no. 15: Monson to Rosebery, 20 January 1893. Cited by Stengers, " Aux origines de Fachoda: l'expédition Monteil," *Revue belge de philologie et d'histoire*, XXXVIII (1960), 379.

19. Andrew, *Théophile Delcassé*, p. 53.

The Comité and the colonial group were not the only organized groups interested in colonial questions. There were older groups like Le Mouvement géographique which had expanded greatly in the 1870's under the leadership of Marquis Chasseloup-Laubat, a former Minister of Marine; [20] and newer groups like the Union coloniale française which was founded in 1893 as " a federation of the leading French business houses with interests in our colonies." [21] The Comité drew support from the older geographical societies, but its base in the Chamber made it much more influential than the geographical movement had ever been. Although the Union coloniale originally declared itself in favor of further expansion, it was dominated more and more during the 1890's by business circles whose primary concern was the economic development of the existing colonies, not expansion into new territory. [22] By 1894 the Union coloniale was draining off the business group support which the Comité had initially enjoyed, and there was a great deal of tension between the two groups.

This tension polarized the colonial movement into two groups, one devoted to economic development, the other to territorial expansion. It is logical to assume that there was a similar polarization in the colonial group between deputies who followed the lead of the Comité and those who agreed with the Union coloniale. At any rate it is certain that the Comité and certain deputies in the colonial faction made up the most dedicated expansionist group in French politics during the last decade of the nineteenth century. It is impossible to write the history of French African policy during this period without taking their influence into consideration.

During the first two years of its existence the Comité concentrated its attention on the African territories adjacent to Lake Chad. [23] The first mission launched by the Comité was headed by Mizon and directed toward this area. This initiative constituted an open challenge to the Ministry of Foreign Affairs policy which

20. See *La grande Encyclopédie* on Chasseloup-Laubat, and Donald Vernon McKay, " Colonialism in the French Geographical Movement: 1871–1881," *Geographical Review*, XXXIII (1943), 214–32.

21. Brunschwig, *Mythes et réalités*, p. 120.

22. *Ibid.*, p. 134.

23. This reflected the influence of Alis, who wrote two books on the subject: *A la Conquête du Tchad* (Paris, 1891) and *Nos Africains* (Paris, 1894). Also see Sanderson, pp. 118–19.

had been embodied in the 5 August 1890 Anglo-French agreement to partition the area.[24] In a pattern which was to be repeated throughout the last decade of the nineteenth century, the Mizon mission was jointly sponsored by the Comité and the colonial department and was in direct contradiction to the policy of the Quai d'Orsay.[25] This foreshadowed the more ambitious missions that were to be launched toward another area of Africa.

In 1892 and 1893 the attention of the Comité began to shift from Lake Chad to an expanse of territory including the Bahr-el-Ghazal and the Upper Nile basin. The strategic center of this region was the ancient fort of Fashoda at the headwaters of the Nile. In the " veritable partition " of Africa which so much concerned the Comité, the area around Fashoda had already been claimed by Great Britain. Historically, it had been a part of the Ottoman Empire and had been controlled by Egypt. Thus, according to the British, it had come within their " sphere of influence " along with the rest of Egypt when Britain occupied Cairo in 1882. In 1885, however, the Upper Nile territory came under the control of the indigenous Mahdist state, and the British had made no effort to re-establish their influence there.[26] This was in large measure because the area had little intrinsic worth. Lord Cromer, the British representative in Cairo, observed that it consisted of " large tracts of useless territory which it would be difficult and costly to administer properly [sic]." [27] Lord Salisbury later summed up his opinion of the Egyptian Sudan in two words— " wretched stuff." [28]

What did the Comité see in the Upper Nile basin which had apparently been overlooked by the British? Why were they interested in an area almost completely devoid of any natural resources and under the control of a hostile native state? There were a number of reasons. The Egyptian Sudan was crucial to the emerging imperial dream of a great French-African empire stretching from Dakar in the west to French Somaliland in the east. French control of this area would prevent Great Britain from

24. BI, Fonds Terrier, 5891, no. 4: d'Arenberg to Alis, 12 September 1890.

25. Sanderson, pp. 118–19.

26. See Peter M. Holt, The Mahdist State in the Sudan, 1881–1898 (Oxford, 1958).

27. Christ Church, Oxford (CCO), Salisbury Papers, A/89: Cabinet Memoranda, 1885–1900, Cromer to Salisbury, 5 November 1897.

28. PRO, FO 78/5051, minute on a report dated 20 October 1898.

dominating the African continent by establishing an empire turning on a north–south axis from Cairo to the Cape of Good Hope. In addition, many members of the Comité became convinced that by occupying the headwaters of the Nile, France could challenge British control in Cairo and settle the Egyptian question in a manner more favorable to France.[29] Thus, the Comité decided in 1893 that a French mission should be launched toward the Upper Nile basin, and for the next two years the group worked to obtain governmental approval for such a project.

Between 1893 and 1896 three missions were in fact prepared and sent toward the Upper Nile—the Monteil mission, the Liotard mission, and the Marchand mission. In gaining approval for these projects the Comité acted primarily through the Undersecretariat, and later through the Ministry of Colonies. The task of launching the first of these missions was made considerably easier for the Comité when Théophile Delcassé became Undersecretary of State for Colonies.

III

After a stormy career as a journalist specializing in foreign affairs, Delcassé was elected deputy from his native department of Ariège in 1889.[30] In his early years Delcassé was a follower of Gambetta and an emotional nationalist of the left.[31] His early writings are almost all polemics directed at times against Germany and at times against Great Britain. *Alerte! Où allons-nous?*, which was the only work other than newspaper articles ever published by Delcassé, vehemently protested the British occupation of Egypt.[32] These writings, as well as Delcassé's first speech in the Chamber, which sought to reconcile colonial expansion with a posture of strength in Europe, impressed expansionists in the Chamber.[33] He had soon established a close relationship with Prince d'Arenberg and was one of the original members of the colonial group.[34] With the group's support, he became Under-

29. See below, pp. 26–27, 39.

30. The most comprehensive study of Delcassé is Andrew's recent book, *Théophile Delcassé and the Making of the Entente Cordiale.*

31. Porter, *Career of Théophile Delcassé*, pp. 12, 13, 17, 18; and Renouvin, *La Politique extérieure de Théophile Delcassé*, p. 3.

32. Théophile Delcassé, *Alerte! Où allons-nous?* (Paris, 1882), pp. 1–34. For a more detailed discussion of Delcassé's early views, see below, pp. 120–26.

33. *Journal officiel*, Chambre, 6 November 1890.

34. MAE, Lettres de Delcassé, Delcassé to Mme. Delcassé, 8 July 1896; *BCAF*, II (July 1892), 16.

secretary of State for Colonies in January 1893. Delcassé accepted the post only on the condition that the colonial department be moved from its quarters in the Ministry of Marine to new offices in the Louvre's Pavillon de Flore.[35]

Soon after Delcassé took power and established himself in his new base of operations overlooking the Arc du Carrousel and the Jardin des Tuileries, he met with Prince d'Arenberg. The directors of the Comité, d'Arenberg told his friend, had decided that a mission should be launched toward the Bahr-el-Ghazal, and that the support of the Pavillon de Flore for the project was imperative.[36] A few days later Delcassé announced that he was in favor of such a project, and on 20 February 1893 the Undersecretary cabled French officials in Libreville to "be prepared to organize [a] mission . . . [which is] to attain [the] Upper Nile basin as soon as possible." [37] In planning what was to become the Monteil mission Delcassé worked very closely with Prince d'Arenberg, even down to outlining how the credits for the project were to be obtained and how much was to be spent.[38] There was, indeed, "close cooperation . . . between the promoters of the Monteil expedition and the directors of the Comité." [39]

Despite the close cooperation between Delcassé and Prince d'Arenberg, it should not be supposed that the Undersecretary for Colonies was a passive instrument of the Comité. The initiative for the project certainly came from the Comité and, within the Comité, from Harry Alis. Toward the end of 1891 or the beginning of 1892 Alis became a paid agent of King Leopold of Belgium. Thereafter, he used his position as secretary-general of the Comité to mold French colonial policy in a form favorable to Belgium and its colony, the Congo State.[40] As conceived by Alis, under the covert influence of the Belgians, a "serious mission toward the Upper Nile" was to be backed by Leopold, which would ultimately result in the partition of the Upper Valley of the Nile between France and the Congo State. Despite pressure

35. A. Duchêne, La Politique coloniale de la France (Paris, 1928), p. 256.

36. Stengers, "Aux origines de Fachoda," p. 444.

37. Ministère des Colonies (MC), Correspondance, Gabon-Congo I, 40b: Delcassé to Chavannes, 20 February 1893. Cited by Sanderson, p. 140.

38. Stengers, "Aux origines de Fachoda," p. 444.

39. Ibid., p. 448.

40. Ibid., passim. Stengers gives a full account of the clandestine relationship between Alis and the Belgians.

from the Comité, Delcassé refused to accept this formulation of a mission toward the Nile.

Delcassé had more soaring ambitions than a mere partitioning of the Nile Valley with the Congo State. On 20 January 1893, Victor Prompt, a French engineer, delivered a paper before the Institut égyptien which argued that a dam could be built across the Upper Nile and used in such a manner as to put Egypt in danger of either drought or rampaging flood waters.[41] Delcassé received an advance copy of this paper, and soon became impressed with its political implications. This event coincided with pressure from the Comité favoring a mission into the area where such a dam could be built. Delcassé accepted the Comité's tactic of sending a mission into the Bahr-el-Ghazal; he rejected their strategy of collaboration with Belgium. Prompt's paper suggested a more far-reaching strategy involving nothing less than reopening the question of British control in Egypt under the implied threat of retaliation.

Rather than seek support for this project at the Ministry of Foreign Affairs, Delcassé approached the President of the Republic, Sadi Carnot. The President, a polytechnician who had graduated with Prompt, was impressed with the scheme, and on 3 May 1893 in the President's study at the Elysée, Delcassé and Carnot persuaded the *officier soudanais* Monteil to head a mission toward the Upper Nile. Carnot then told Monteil in no uncertain terms the goal of the mission: "*Il faut occuper Fachoda.*"[42] On 10 June an advance party of the Monteil expedition departed from France for Africa.

The French Ministry of Foreign Affairs was completely bypassed during this entire moment in the decision-making process. In June the Minister of Foreign Affairs, Jules Develle, complained that he had learned of the Monteil mission by reading the morning papers rather than through any official communication of the Undersecretariat for Colonies. In July he wrote that he still had "no indication of the composition or objective of the Monteil mission."[43] This slighting of the Quai d'Orsay set a pattern

41. Victor Prompt, "Soudan nilotique," *Bulletin de l'Institut égyptien*, III (1893), 71-116. See also Langer, *Diplomacy of Imperialism*, pp. 127–28, for a discussion of the content and effects of Prompt's paper.

42. Parfait L. Monteil, *Souvenirs vécus* (Paris, 1924), pp. 65–68.

43. MC, Afrique IV, 43: Develle to Delcassé, 23 July 1893. Cited in Stengers, "Aux origines de Fachoda," p. 449. Also see Afrique III, 19: Mission Monteil.

which was to become almost a tradition in Upper Nile policy in France.

Delcassé fell from office in December 1893. There followed a period of confusion and indecision during which the Monteil mission hung in the balance. In May 1894 when Delcassé returned to the Pavillon de Flore with the full rank of minister in the Dupuy cabinet, he found that Monteil was still nowhere near Fashoda. This was a situation Delcassé was determined to alter.

IV

Gabriel Hanotaux, the new Minister of Foreign Affairs in the Dupuy cabinet, was just as determined that the Monteil mission or any other French mission never reach the Upper Nile. Hanotaux had never held political office. Rather he had risen to prominence as a career official at the Quai d'Orsay, and was steeped in the ministry's traditions. By temperament and training, he was more concerned with maintaining good relations with the European powers than with African adventures.

Hanotaux opposed a mission toward the Upper Nile on two counts. First of all, he was genuinely concerned with improving relations with Great Britain, which had been strained by the Siamese crisis of 1893, and he feared that a challenge to Britain on the Upper Nile would completely destroy any hope for an Anglo-French entente.[44] Further, Hanotaux believed that French occupation of Fashoda would contradict traditional French policy which recognized " the integrity of the Ottoman Empire." [45] The tradition-minded Quai d'Orsay had continued to recognize the Sultan as the legal ruler of Egypt long after all vestiges of Turkish power there had been destroyed. To send a mission to the Upper Nile would be a contradiction, since France " protests constantly against occupation or similar acts which constitute a patent breach of the law in these areas." [46] In this way Hanotaux put his depart-

44. It is often argued that Hanotaux was pro-German and anglophobe, but the Papiers Hanotaux reveal that he favored closer relations with Great Britain. See the discussion of this point in Georges Dethan, " Les Papiers de Gabriel Hanotaux et le proclamation de l'entente franco-russe (1895–1897)," *Revue d'histoire diplomatique*, LXXX (1966), 205–13. See also the account of Hanotaux's attempt to come to an agreement with England in A. J. P. Taylor, " Prelude to Fashoda: The Question of the Upper Nile," *Economic History Review*, LXV (1950), 52–80.

45. Hanotaux's words cited by Sanderson, p. 191.

46. MAE, Mémoires et documents, Afrique, CXXXIX. Cited by Stengers, " Aux origines de Fachoda," p. 381.

ment on record as being opposed to a forward policy on the Nile.

Hanotaux's policy was dealt a heavy blow by the announcement of the Anglo-Congolese agreement of 1894. King Leopold, after finding that even his agent Alis could not secure French agreement for a partition of the Nile Valley, had made the same proposition to the British with much greater success. In June 1894 the terms of the Anglo-Congolese agreement which provided for the division of the Upper Nile were made public. There was a general outcry, and the colonial group led a chorus of protest in the Chamber. After a lengthy discourse on the traditional rights of the Sultan and Egypt in the Valley of the Upper Nile which questioned Britain's right to dispose of territory not legally controlled by her, Hanotaux argued that he considered the Anglo-Congolese agreement null and void. Then, with a flourish, he added a dramatic statement which was clearly intended to quiet an aroused Chamber:

> My colleague, the Minister of Colonies, has given the necessary orders for the commanding officer in Upper Ubangi to return to his post immediately. The first detachments of his mission have arrived on the scene. They will be reinforced without delay . . . . The head of the mission . . . will leave France shortly by steamer. The Chamber will understand if I say no more on this matter.[47]

The Chamber responded by an overwhelming vote on the order of the day drafted by Etienne and Deloncle which pledged the government to safeguard French rights in Africa. A measure of the temper of the Chamber was the vote of one million francs " for the defense of French interests in Africa " which came after a request by Delcassé on 18 June.[48]

This looked very much like a full-scale endorsement of a drive to re-establish French interests in the Nilotic Sudan. Acting on this assumption, Delcassé cabled Libreville on the day following Hanotaux's speech that Monteil and his men would leave France in late June.[49] Monteil's departure, however, did not occur until 16 July. The delay was undoubtedly caused by a conflict between Delcassé and Hanotaux concerning the form of Monteil's orders.[50]

47. *Journal officiel*, Chambre, 7 June 1894.
48. *Ibid.*, 18 and 20 June 1894.
49. MC, Correspondance, Gabon-Congo, I, 45b: Delcassé to Libreville, 8 June 1894. Cited by Sanderson, p. 188.
50. Sanderson, p. 188.

Delcassé probably argued that the goal of the Monteil mission had already been decided, but Hanotaux insisted on issuing a new set of instructions which categorically prohibited Monteil from penetrating to the basin of the Nile " so that the question of the Egyptian Sudan remains open and completely reserved." [51] In a private conversation Hanotaux required of Monteil " a formal commitment . . . that he would never send a body of soldiers or even a single man into the Nile basin." [52] Thus, while presenting a hard line before the Chamber, Hanotaux had moved behind the scenes to completely alter the character of the Monteil mission and reduce it to the task of " consolidating " the French position in the Upper Ubangi.[53] This was the last time that Hanotaux ever succeeded in overruling the Ministry of Colonies on a question of Upper Nile policy.

A month after these events, Delcassé, in what appears to have been a calculated attempt to assert the independence of his newly created ministry, summarily ordered Monteil to the Ivory Coast rather than the Upper Ubangi.[54] Evidently the Monteil mission was no longer of any use to Delcassé since its scope had been so effectively limited by the formal intervention of Hanotaux. Almost immediately Delcassé began to plan a new Upper Nile project. Monteil's successor was to be Victor Liotard, a colonial administrator who had served under de Brazza, and who was conveniently in Paris in September 1894.

Obstacles to gaining government approval for the Liotard mission were much greater than those Delcassé had faced in 1893. Delcassé still enjoyed the support of the Comité and the colonial group, but his ally at the Elysée had now been eliminated by an anarchist's bullet. The new President—brooding, neurotic Casimir-Périer—had been opposed to the Monteil mission earlier; [55] now in September he was not disposed to give the kind of full-scale support which Carnot had given Delcassé, and which had made possible the bypassing of the Quai d'Orsay in 1893. Hanotaux had forced Delcassé to give way on the matter of orders to Monteil and was determined that the question not be reopened.

51. *DDF*, XI, Delcassé to Monteil, 13 July 1894.
52. *Ibid.*, minute by Hanotaux, 12 July 1894.
53. *Ibid.*, Delcassé to Monteil, 13 July 1894.
54. MC, Afrique III, 19b, Delcassé to Monteil, 14 August 1894. Cited by Sanderson, p. 189.
55. Sanderson, pp. 151–52.

One course of action was left open to Delcassé; if he wanted to gain official approval for the Liotard mission, he would have to undermine Hanotaux's personal position within the cabinet, rally a majority of his ministerial colleagues, and override the objections of the Minister of Foreign Affairs.

In normal times this course of action would have been out of the question. During the Third Republic the cabinet generally accepted the views of the Minister of Foreign Affairs in the area of external policy. But in the fall of 1894 France was on the eve of a long period of abnormal times: on 27 September a bordereau was brought to the rue Sainte Dominique offices of the army's Section de Statistique, the center of French intelligence and counter-intelligence. On the basis of this evidence, suspicion soon rose that Captain Alfred Dreyfus was guilty of supplying military secrets to a German agent. The *affaire* which was to bear the name of Dreyfus had begun.

V

The Ministry of Foreign Affairs was almost immediately in-volved in the Dreyfus affair. On 11 October 1894, General Mer-cier, the Minister of War, called together those ministers whom he believed should be consulted about the case. Prime Minister Dupuy, Minister of Justice Guerin, and Hanotaux were present. Of these, only Hanotaux opposed pressing the case further.[56] He categorically declared: " If you have no proof beyond that written message and a similarity in handwriting, I am opposed to any legal action, or even any investigation." [57] Hanotaux feared that any attempt to press the matter further would only lead to increased tension in Franco-German relations, and he urgently warned that a dramatic espionage trial could provoke the " gravest international difficulties." Hanotaux, therefore, tried to convince a number of ministers that the "national interest" would be jeopardized if further steps were taken against Dreyfus.[58]

---

56. Douglas Johnson, *France and the Dreyfus Affair* (London, 1966), p. 18.
57. Maurice Paléologue, *Journal de l'affaire Dreyfus 1894–1899; l'affaire Drey-fus et le Quai d'Orsay* (Paris, 1955), p. 3.
58. Archives Nationales (AN), 53 AP: Papiers de Sallintin (Conseiller de la cour de cassation concernant le procès Dreyfus). This records Hanotaux's testimony in 1898 to the effect that his actions at this juncture were prompted by fear of the diplomatic consequences of a possible trial. See also Paléologue, *Journal de l'affaire Dreyfus*, p. 3. T. M. Iiams, *Dreyfus, Diplomatists and the Dual Alliance: Gabriel*

Hanotaux's views were quite different from those of his colleagues. On 1 November the entire Dupuy cabinet was informed of the case. The mood of the group is evident from Delcassé's response: " If these are the facts, and unfortunately they most probably are, there is no place for pity, and we must apply every severity of the law." [59] Thus, in terms of cabinet politics, Hanotaux was increasingly isolated.

Delcassé seized upon this moment, when the prestige and personal position of the Foreign Minister were at a low ebb, to press for cabinet approval of the new Upper Nile expedition. He chose once again work through the President of the Republic. Casimir-Périer had earlier been opposed to a forward policy on the Upper Nile, but now, because of a growing personal hostility for Hanotaux resulting from the Foreign Minister's failure to consult the Elysée on foreign policy questions, the President was disposed to listen to Delcassé.[60]

At the cabinet meeting of 17 November Casimir-Périer pressed for approval of the Liotard mission. Delcassé followed the President's presentation with an exposition of the views of the Ministry of Colonies on the subject. Only a little more than two weeks had passed since the cabinet had overruled Hanotaux and decided that the Ministry of War should proceed against Dreyfus. Now the Foreign Minister was outvoted on a question which was directly within his area of competence, and the decision to launch the Liotard mission was made " *sur les observations de M. Delcassé.*" [61]

The strictly enforced custom of keeping no written record of cabinet proceedings makes it difficult to determine exactly why Hanotaux was overruled on 17 November. It is possible that the cabinet was sympathetic to a policy of expansion, and that the Liotard mission was accepted on the basis of its own merits and in view of the fact that Franco-British negotiations on the Nile had broken down.[62] It seems more likely, however, that members of the cabinet had no clear position on foreign policy questions, and that they followed Delcassé's lead at this time because Hano-

Hanotaux at the Quai d'Orsay (*1894–1898*) (Paris-Geneva, 1962), gives a cursory account of Hanotaux's views on the Dreyfus affair.

59. MAE, Lettres de Delcassé, Delcassé to Mme. Delcassé, 1 November 1894.

60. See Hanotaux, " Carnets," ed. G.-L. Jaray, *Revue des deux mondes*, April 1949, pp. 385–403.

61. *DDF*, XI, nos. 285 and 305.

62. See Andrew, *Théophile Delcassé*, pp. 43–44.

taux's prestige and influence had been damaged by his position on the Dreyfus case. It is at any rate certain that when the cabinet deliberated French policy toward the Upper Nile, it decided in favor of the Pavillon de Flore and against the Quai d'Orsay. This was a clear victory for Delcassé. On the following day the Comité and colonial group, " as a tribute to the services rendered by him to the cause of our colonial expansion," presented a special award to the young minister in obvious tribute to his latest success.[63]

What was a victory for Delcassé was a crushing defeat for Hanotaux with far-reaching repercussions. The " cabinet decision of 17 November," concludes Sanderson, " was a serious defeat . . . . Hanotaux' authority in African affairs never recovered from these initial set-backs. His non-political status deprived him of a French minister's strongest weapon: the threat to bring down the Government by taking into opposition one of the parliamentary groups upon whose precarious co-operation the life of a French Cabinet depended." [64] Hanotaux never again questioned the two decisions which he had opposed in November 1894. He never again challenged the Ministry of War concerning the Dreyfus affair; he never again effectively opposed the Ministry of Colonies on policy toward the Upper Nile. By March 1896 the British ambassador in Paris could truly write that although Hanotaux was " undoubtedly a strong and most intelligent man," he had become in African questions, " more of a mouthpiece than a free agent." [65] The domestic political situation of November 1894 probably played a large role in creating this situation.

Since 1893, the colonialists and the continentalists, the Pavillon de Flore and the Quai d'Orsay, had been in conflict over the question of French policy toward the Upper Nile. By the end of 1894 the colonialists had the upper hand and under their influence events were moving inexorably in the direction of the Fashoda crisis.

63. *BCAF*, IV (December 1894). The award itself embodied all the self-conscious arrogance of European imperialism: a sculpture called " The Explorer " depicting " a white man raising his hand with a gesture of hope and pride pointing out the heavens to a young black man kneeling before him."

64. Sanderson, p. 208.

65. PRO, FO 27/3274, no. 41: Dufferin to Salisbury, 3 March 1896. Cited by Sanderson, p. 208.

Chapter II

DOMESTIC POLITICS AND THE MARCHAND MISSION, I:
1895

Soon after the November cabinet meeting which approved the Liotard mission, Anglo-French relations deteriorated. During the first months of 1895, almost all hope for an amicable settlement of Anglo-French claims on the Upper Nile disappeared in the heat of parliamentary oratory on both sides of the channel.

In January 1895 Harry Alis used the *Bulletin* to reiterate publicly that the Comité was in favor of French penetration to the Upper Nile. France, Alis argued, should " take up a position on the Nile that would block new encroachments by the English." [1] The well-known explorer-colonialist de Brazza echoed this call the following month, and added that an advance into the Nile was the only way to resolve the entire Egyptian question. In the Chamber these pronouncements evoked a response among those deputies who were closely associated with the colonial movement in France: impassioned anti-British speeches by Flourens and Deloncle reiterated the demand for a mission to the Upper Nile designed to pressure the British into reopening the Egyptian question.[2]

These statements from the floor of the Chamber evoked a response in the House of Commons. In an early March editorial which was extremely critical of the British government, *The Times* raised the question of French activities directed toward the region of the Upper Nile.[3] This was followed by a vehement speech in Commons by Sir Ellis Ashmead-Bartlett. He demanded an immediate response to the statements made by Deloncle and de Brazza in the form of a government declaration " that the whole Nile

1. *BCAF*, V (January 1895), 83.
2. Jules Cocheris, *Situation internationale de l'Egypte et du Soudan* (Paris, 1903), p. 414; Sanderson, p. 212.
3. Cocheris, *Situation internationale*, p. 415.

waterway is within the British sphere and that no foreign occupation of the Nile will be permitted." [4]

Toward the end of March reports reached London of successful French advances on the Niger,[5] and the fear grew in Commons that France might present Britain with a similar fait accompli on the Nile. On 28 March Ashmead-Bartlett repeated his demand for an official pronouncement on the subject. He argued that there was a race between Britain and France for "trans-African dominion," with the British working from north to south and the French from east to west. If France presented Britain with a fait accompli on the Nile, he concluded, the British position in Egypt would be rendered "untenable." [6]

By raising the Egyptian question, the Commons debate struck a vital nerve in British imperial policy. Britain had moved into Egypt in large measure to protect the old empire in India, and much of British policy in Africa was premised on the need to protect their foothold in Cairo and therefore keep the lifeline of the Suez Canal open to their possessions in the Far East. According to Robinson and Gallagher, the "decisive motive behind late-Victorian strategy in Africa was to protect the all-important stakes in India and the East." [7] Whether or not the Egyptian question was the most significant factor for all British policy in Africa, it certainly played an important role in attitudes toward the Egyptian Sudan.[8]

This is clearly shown in the government response to the Commons debate of 28 March. The Undersecretary of State for Foreign Affairs, Sir Edward Grey, discounted rumors that France was advancing toward the Upper Nile. But under pressure from the floor of Commons, he added that the "advance of a French expedition under secret instructions, right from the other side of Africa, into a territory over which our claims have been known for so long, would not be merely an inconsistent and unexpected act, but it must be perfectly well known to the French Government that it would be an unfriendly act, and would be so viewed

4. Hansard (Commons), 4th ser., XXXII, 394. Cited by Sanderson, p. 213.

5. See Newbury, "French Policy on the Niger," pp. 16–26.

6. Hansard, XXXII, 388–403. Cited by Sanderson, p. 214.

7. Ronald Robinson and John Gallagher, *Africa and the Victorians: The Official Mind of Imperialism* (London, 1961), p. 464.

8. For a critique of the Robinson-Gallagher thesis, see Stengers, "L'Impérialisme colonial," pp. 469–91.

by England." [9] This statement, which came to be called the Grey Declaration, was not a premeditated formulation of cabinet policy.[10] It was approved by Prime Minister Rosebery and then by Salisbury, however, it became the basis of British policy toward France and the Upper Nile.

The Grey Declaration was important for another reason: it marked a break with traditional cabinet diplomacy. By declaring British policy in Commons rather than through normal diplomatic channels, the Grey Declaration foreshadowed the age of " diplomacy by public warning" and struck the "first note of the hysteria which was to overwhelm foreign policy towards the end of the century." [11]

The hysteria was infectious. Joseph Chamberlain, the man who was soon to become Minister of Colonies in Britain, reiterated the phrase " unfriendly act " three times in an ensuing polemical speech directed at France. Another parliamentarian labeled the statement " a quasi-declaration of war against France." [12] Rather than deter French colonial circles, the Grey Declaration only reinforced their conviction that Britain was the " eternal rival " and was determined to exclude France from the entire continent of Africa.[13] The French ambassador in London called the speech a " *coup de théâtre*," and even Hanotaux believed that the Grey Declaration was " an unscrupulous attempt to assert by parliamentary demonstration a claim which France still hotly disputed." [14]

Hanotaux, however, had not given up hope of dealing with the question in the quiet language of diplomacy. He realized that the Grey Declaration represented a hardening of the British line, and that any French moves in the Upper Nile would have serious consequences. He therefore renewed his efforts to come to some kind of understanding with Britain on the question, and in April and May Franco-British relations improved somewhat.[15] Hanotaux

9. Hansard, XXXII, 403–407. Cited by Sanderson, p. 214.

10. R. R. James, *Rosebery: A Biography of Archibald Philip, Fifth Earl of Rosebery* (London, 1963), p. 374.

11. Robinson and Gallagher, *Africa and the Victorians*, pp. 335-36.

12. Hansard, XXXII, 407–9, 416–20. Cited by Sanderson, p. 217.

13. See below, pp. 38–39, for Marchand's response, typical of the colonial milieu.

14. Sanderson, p. 217.

15. For a complete account of these negotiations, see John D. Hargreaves, " *Entente Manquée*: Anglo-French Relations 1895–1896," *Cambridge Historical Journal*, XI (1953), 65–92, and Sanderson, pp. 217–24.

went so far as to propose a project for neutralizing the whole Nile Valley and placing it under the control of an international commission.[16] It was therefore not unwelcome news at the Quai d'Orsay that the Liotard mission, after encountering insurmountable practical difficulties, had come to a near-standstill far short of Fashoda. If events had continued in the direction in which they were headed in the spring of 1895, there might never have been a Fashoda crisis.[17]

By the summer, however, the Comité de l'Afrique française had learned of Liotard's difficulties and of the Quai d'Orsay's attempts at rapprochement with the British Foreign Office at Whitehall. The leaders of the Comité were determined to reverse this trend, and the chosen agent of their intentions was a young officer in the infantry marine: Captain Jean-Baptiste Marchand.

II

Marchand's first contact with the Comité de l'Afrique française was in the summer of 1893. The ambitious Marchand had gained approval of the colonial department for a " mission of geographic and commercial exploration " to the Ivory Coast. Marchand wrote a warm letter introducing himself to Prince d'Arenberg and sent it, along with a lengthy *rapport* of the Ivory Coast mission, in the hope that the " aid and concourse of the Comité " would be forthcoming for his project.[18] The following day Marchand presented himself at the headquarters of the Comité on rue de la Ville l'Evêque, where he met Prince d'Arenberg, Auguste Terrier, and other important members of the group. This marked the beginning of a long and mutually beneficial relationship between the explorer-soldier and the Comité; thereafter Marchand became an avid reader of the *Bulletin* and one of the group's most active and influential members.[19] Terrier became, in Marchand's mind,

16. Sanderson, p. 269.
17. Renouvin, " L'Expédition de Fachoda," p. 189.
18. BI, Fonds Terrier, 5930: Mission J-B Marchand en Côte d'Ivoire, 1893–1894, Marchand to Prince d'Arenberg, August 1893.
19. There is an entire dossier of letters from Marchand to Terrier dealing with the tactics and politics of the Comité: BI, Fonds Terrier, 5904: Correspondance d'Auguste Terrier. See especially Marchand to Terrier (n. d.), where Marchand requests that copies of the *Bulletin* be sent to a long list of career officials at the Ministries of Marine and War; and Marchand to Terrier (1897), where Marchand enthusiastically thanks Terrier for sending the *Bulletin* to him in Africa.
Some of the letters in this dossier have been reprinted: " Lettres du commandant

a " *cher maître et ami*," [20] and Prince d'Arenberg earned his " profound respect." [21] In 1897 Marchand summed up his views in a letter written to Terrier from the heart of Africa:

> . . . I sincerely believe that there is a small group of men for whom the colonial question is not merely an excuse for banquets and speeches and extravagant lectures. But there are only a very few of you who share these views and I know almost all of you—you are for the most part in the Comité de l'Afrique française.[22]

It was at this time that Marchand first became interested in the Upper Nile project.[23] Even after setting out on his mission through Africa, the idea haunted him. While in the Ivory Coast, he served with Monteil. The older man told Marchand the history of the first Upper Nile mission and encouraged him to renew the noble work which he had first attempted.[24] When Marchand returned to Paris in the summer of 1895, he was convinced that he should head a new Fashoda expedition.

In June 1895 Marchand obtained an interview with the Minister of Foreign Affairs.[25] In an effort to bury the scheme without offending a representative of the colonial army, Hanotaux politely suggested that the project be written up and submitted to the Ministry of Colonies. Marchand took Hanotaux at his word, and prepared a report entitled " Mission du Congo-Nil, le Bahr el Ghazal." [26]

Marchand's lengthy report, twenty-one $11 \times 16\frac{1}{2}$-inch pages and a detailed carte, is divided into five " *titres*." The first deals with the geography of the area, and the historical background up to

Marchand à Guillaume Grandidier," ed. M.-A. Menier, *Revue d'histoire des colonies*, XLV (1958), 61–108. It is certain that the letters printed here were sent to Terrier, not Grandidier. They are in the Fonds Terrier, and internal evidence confirms that Marchand was writing to Terrier. The editor of this printed collection somehow confused Grandidier, secretary-general of Le Mouvement géographique, with Terrier, secretary-general of the Comité.

20. BI, Fonds Terrier, 5904, Marchand to Terrier, n. d.

21. Bibliothèque Nationale (BN), nouvelle acquisition française (n. a. fr.) 24327: Eugène Etienne, Correspondance, 1887–1921, Marchand to Etienne, 11 December 1898.

22. BI, Fonds Terrier, 5904, Marchand to Terrier, 25 November 1897.

23. Jacques Delebecque, *Vie du Général Marchand* (Paris, 1936), p. 69.

24. Monteil, *Souvenirs vécus*, pp. 115–16, 121.

25. Marchand, *Le Matin*, 20 June 1905.

26. MC, Afrique III, 32a, no. 1.

the time of European penetration. *Titre* IV is a detailed projection of the personnel and equipment needed to outfit the mission, and *titre* V is a financial projection of the cost of the mission over a period of thirty months. The most important sections are *titres* II and III, which outline the strategy and tactics of the project.

Marchand began *titre* II, " La question du Nil au point de vue politique," with quotations from the Grey Declaration of 28 March 1895 to the effect that the combined rights of Britain and Egypt apply to the " *totalité de la Vallée du Nil.*" Marchand depicted what he considered long-range British strategy by drawing a map of Africa and crossing the continent with two heavy black lines. One extended from Alexandria to the Cape; the other traversed the continent from Lagos to Mombassa. The two lines intersected in the Upper Nile Valley, and Marchand went on to argue that this area was crucial to the completion of Britain's scheme for expansion in Africa. He labeled this strategy the " English theory of the African cross."

As a counterstrategy for France, Marchand proposed the " more modest French theory " of an empire traversing northern Africa from Dakar to French Somaliland. He envisioned a mission to Fashoda which would strike at the heart of the " English theory of the African cross " by countering both the north–south and the east–west thrusts of British expansion. At the same time, a French presence in the Egyptian Sudan would insure French influence in a broad expanse of northern Africa from the Atlantic to French Somaliland and would weaken British control in Cairo by forcing the reopening of the Egyptian question. Marchand clearly understood the implications of his project. He underlined the following sentence of the Grey Declaration: " Such a move on the part of France would in fact be a hostile act (*acte d'hostilité*), and the French government knows quite well that we would so interpret it." [27] Rather than deter France from acting, Grey's words only incensed French imperialist circles. Exclaimed Marchand: " And it's a Whig who threatens us from the height of the English rostrum and with his ministerial authority." In fact, Marchand expected the British line to harden still further. He predicted that

27. Sanderson goes to some length to show that in the context of the original Grey Declaration the words " unfriendly act " did not carry the same menacing connotation which they acquired in 1898, pp. 215–17. Marchand's translation of these words as " *acte d'hostilité* " indicates that the meaning was clear enough to the French.

the "crushing victory" of the Tories in the British elections of 1895 was a signal for a very active renewal of British expansion. "Will we allow ourselves to be intimidated?" he asked.

Marchand's determined "*non*" was to be embodied in his mission to Fashoda. He saw his project as the only alternative to the complete isolation and ultimate loss of French possessions on the African continent. Just as France had been excluded from North America in the eighteenth century, so would the "eternal rival" expel her from Africa unless there was vigorous action. In addition to insuring France's future in Africa, the "Mission du Congo-Nil" would end Britain's "prolonged and illegal occupation of Egypt." This was Marchand's strategy.

Marchand outlined the tactics he envisioned in *titre* III, "Projet du mission." He argued that a small group of French officers, leading perhaps two hundred African troops, could penetrate from Brazzaville to Fashoda in about thirty months. Contacts could then be established with the leaders of the Mahdist State, the men whose armies had destroyed Gordon's expedition and excluded the British from the Egyptian Sudan in the 1880's.[28] The Mahdists, Marchand believed, were the "natural allies" of France, and would act as a buffer between a small French force at Fashoda and the Anglo-Egyptian army further down the Nile.

Except for the tactical innovation of dealing with the Mahdists, and the rather elaborate development of the "English theory of the African cross," there was very little new in Marchand's report. It was simply a revival of the ideas which proponents of the Upper Nile project had advocated at least since 1893. Only Marchand's arrogant style and real note of urgency set it apart from previous presentations of the idea. This is not at all strange, because the Comité had first introduced Marchand to the idea and was involved in getting official approval for the new mission in the summer of 1895. Prince d'Arenberg later admitted that his group "had purposely instigated, planned and started the Marchand expedition . . ."[29]

28. See Holt, "The Sudanese Mahdia and the Outside World, 1881–1889," *Bulletin of the School of Oriental and African Studies*, XXI (1958), 276–90.

29. Douglas F. Dawson, *A Soldier-Diplomat* (London, 1927), pp. 243–44. See also *BCAF*, V (June 1895), 188; (July 1895), 221–22; (August 1895), 235–42. In June 1895 d'Arenberg organized a Comité de l'Egypte to rally public support for a forward policy on the Upper Nile. The July issue of the *BCAF* defined the new Comité's goals as follows: "*Notre oeuvre consisterer à amener l'évacuation militaire de l'Egypte . . .*" This was also the goal of the Marchand mission.

Just as on previous occasions, the Comité gained access to official circles through the Ministry of Colonies. Marchand and the Comité were working closely with Ernest Roume, a career official at the Pavillon de Flore and head of the Bureau de l'Afrique, a key position there. Marchand gave the report personally to Roume on 11 September, and it was then quickly brought to the attention of the responsible minister, Chautemps.[30] The Minister of Colonies immediately realized he was considering a sensitive subject with dangerous implications. Quite responsibly he forwarded the report to the Quai d'Orsay and requested Hanotaux's views " on a question which deals more with general foreign policy than with purely colonial interests." [31]

Marchand once again discussed his project with the Minister of Foreign Affairs, and years later he asserted that Hanotaux was at that time " ready to sign " an approval of his mission.[32] This is very unlikely. In the fall of 1895 Hanotaux was in no mood to approve a new initiative toward the Upper Nile. Although he had submitted to the will of the Dupuy cabinet in November 1894, he had never ceased to search for an alternate policy which would not involve such a dramatic challenge to Great Britain.[33] In fact all that the Foreign Minister did was to put off the decision once again by proposing an interdepartmental conference on the subject.[34]

Before the proposed conference between the two ministries could meet, however, domestic politics intervened to alter the course of events.

III

On 28 October 1895 the Ribot ministry fell following a violent interpellation on the government's handling of the Carmaux glass workers' strike.[35] Then the delicate game of cabinet-building was played through and the fate of the Marchand mission hung in the balance until the winners were announced.

30. MC, Afrique III, 32a, no. 5: Marchand to Roume, 26 January 1896.
31. DDF, XII, no. 152: Chautemps to Hanotaux, 21 September 1895.
32. Marchand, Le Matin, 20 June 1905.
33. See Courcel's private letters to Hanotaux, " France et Angleterre en 1895," Revue historique, CCXII (1954), 39–60; and Hargreaves, " Entente Manquée," 65–92.
34. DDF, XII, no. 197: note pour le ministre, 13 November 1895.
35. Notes personnelles de Félix Faure, 1894–99 (NPFF), IV: " Crise du 28 Octobre 1895," October 1895.

Félix Faure, Casimir-Périer's successor at the Elysée, consulted Brisson on 29 October.[36] Brisson, "*radical de strict observance*," [37] argued that the results of the elections of 1893 had never been registered at the level of cabinet formation, and that only this could explain the successive failures of four " moderate " governments. Since 1893, Brisson continued, there had been a radical majority in the Chamber, and even without socialist or *rallié* support, a " radical government could count 280 votes on bad days, 320 votes on good days." Thus any other combination would be reversed.

Faure was told that there was a host of talented radicals ready to assume cabinet-level positions. Léon Bourgeois would become Prime Minister; Lockroy, Minister of Marine; Cavaignac, Minister of War; and, Faure was assured, talented men would be found to assume responsibility at other strategic ministries. Bourgeois was charged to form a cabinet.

Difficulties arose when Bourgeois began to search for qualified persons willing to accept responsibility at the Ministries of Foreign Affairs and Colonies. Hanotaux was asked to remain at the Quai d'Orsay, and when he hesitated, Faure arranged for Bourgeois and Hanotaux to meet face to face to discuss the problem. The Foreign Minister told Bourgeois that he had insurmountable differences with Lockroy and Cavaignac over French policy toward Madagascar, but behind this façade were deeper motives.

Hanotaux, in collusion with Freycinet, a moderate deputy, had decided to destroy the radical cabinet at its inception by refusing to participate in the new combination. These tactics were based partly on illusion—Hanotaux's proud belief that he was a *grand commis* like Richelieu and Vergennes, untainted by the exigencies of Chamber politics and indispensable to the nation [38]—and partly on the solid observation that there were few French parliamentarians, especially among the radicals, with much experience or sustained interest in foreign affairs.

Bourgeois consulted his colleagues in the Chamber, but no one

36. NPFF, V: " Formation et débuts du cabinet Bourgeois," October 1895–January 1896. The following account of the formation of the Bourgeois cabinet is taken almost completely from this source. As President, Faure was in an excellent position to know the details of the process. See Philip Williams, " Crisis in France: A Political Institution," *Cambridge Journal*, XXXV (October 1963), 36–50.

37. Chastenet, *Histoire de la Troisième République*, p. 75.

38. Sanderson, p. 191.

would volunteer for Foreign Affairs. He then pressed a number of professional diplomats and was refused.[39] On 31 October, after two days of frantic conferences and hurried telegrams, the radical experiment was in danger of destruction at the preparatory stage. The enemies of the radicals had correctly observed Bourgeois' weak point, and were on the eve of success. Even Bourgeois feared that he was defeated.[40]

It was at this crucial juncture that Marcelin Berthelot, senator and distinguished chemist, hinted that he would be happy to be Minister of Foreign Affairs. He had orginally been slated to be Minister of Education, but when he told Bourgeois that although he had no diplomatic experience, he was a member of numerous international scientific societies, including two in Russia, the desperate Bourgeois was impressed. When the prospective Prime Minister suggested the idea to Faure, it was very coldly received.

Bourgeois could find no substitute and, grasping at straws, arranged for Faure to meet Berthelot in the hope that Faure might alter his opinion. Berthelot pleased the President by declaring himself for " the maintenance of close relations with Russia " and a " clear, equitable, loyal and conciliatory policy" toward the Vatican. Faure was less impressed with the prospective minister's views on Germany. " As I spoke to him of my preoccupations vis-à-vis Germany," Faure wrote, " he entered into a medical discussion about the health of the Emperor." The astonished Faure learned that Berthelot was following the cardiac problems of William II with the care of a concerned doctor in a scientific effort to forecast future German policy: " If the abscess bursts out on the surface, there will be nothing to fear, Europe will remain at peace; if, on the other hand, the abscess bursts on the inside, there will be war! " It was almost like saying, Faure concluded, " that diplomacy could be usefully replaced by surgery." Only very reluctantly did the President—*faute de mieux*—approve Bourgeois' candidate for Minister of Foreign Affairs.[41]

The decrees for the new ministry were signed late in the evening on 1 November,[42] but only three days later did Bourgeois persuade Guieysse, an academician like Berthelot, to accept the portfolio

39. Chastenet, *Histoire de la Troisième République*, p. 85.
40. NPFF, " Formation et débuts."
41. *Ibid.*
42. In order to avoid 2 November: " Jour des morts."

of the Minister of Colonies. Guieysse's specialty was the study
of ancient Egypt; but nothing in his previous work had prepared
him for dealing with policy questions related to the Egyptian
Sudan of the nineteenth century. He was, like his colleague at
the Quai d'Orsay, somewhat bewildered by the various decisions
demanded by the permanent officials of his ministry.

Guieysse was hardly given time to learn his way around the
Pavillon de Flore before Roume thrust Marchand's " Mission du
Congo-Nil " into his hands. On 8 November a departmental note
had been sent to the new Minister of Foreign Affairs urgently
requesting a decision on the Marchand project.[43] Two days later
Marchand submitted a " Note analytique et complémentaire "
which Roume communicated to both new ministers. This presented
Marchand's project forcefully and more succinctly than the long-
winded original report.[44]

On 13 November the Direction Politique of the Ministry of
Foreign Affairs joined Marchand and the Ministry of Colonies in
pressing Berthelot for a decision on the problem.[45] The permanent
officials of both ministries renewed the idea of an interdepartmental meeting, but it was never held. On 21 November, at a
meeting of the cabinet, Guieysse passed Berthelot a note urgently
requesting formal approval for the " new mission." [46] Everything
depended on the decision of Marcelin Berthelot.

Berthelot had proved himself completely unable to cope with
the responsibilities of his new position. A few days after the
formation of the Bourgeois cabinet, the new Foreign Minister
was grief-stricken by the death of his daughter. He neglected the
customary diplomatic receptions at the Quai d'Orsay. At cabinet
meetings he " limited himself to listening and to taking down on
scraps of paper crude notes that he was unable to decipher the
next day." [47] On 20 February Berthelot informed Bourgeois of his
desire to resign, but no one could be found to replace him. Months
later Bourgeois himself was forced to take over as Minister of
Foreign Affairs, but in late November 1895 an inexperienced and
saddened man with only " very vague ideas " about foreign policy
gave the colonial department a formal letter approving the

43. *DDF*, XII, no. 190: note du Ministre des Colonies, 8 November 1895.
44. MC., Afrique III, 32a, no. 2.
45. *DDF*, XII, no. 197: note pour le ministre, 13 November 1895.
46. *Ibid.*, no. 210: note de M. Guieysse, 21 November 1895.
47. NPFF, " Formation et débuts."

Marchand mission without ever raising the matter at a cabinet meeting.[48] It was to be the only explicit written approval that the Quai d'Orsay ever issued for the project. In another situation Faure wrote that Berthelot had accepted his ideas " like a school boy "; [49] in much the same way the eminent scientist approved the project that was to bring France to the very brink of war three years later. Although the 30 November note contained reservations, Berthelot concluded the letter by saying that, as he understood it, he gave his " entire adhesion " to the project.[50] In all future debates Berthelot's confused reservations were forgotten, and Marchand and his supporters simply reiterated that they had the " entire adhesion " of the Ministry of Foreign Affairs for their project.

48. *Ibid.*
49. *Ibid.*
50. MC, Afrique III, 32a, no. 3: Berthelot to Guieysse, 30 November 1895. The original carries the title: " Occupation du Haut Oubangui—Mission dans le Bahr-el gazel [*sic*]." On Berthelot's reservations, see below, pp. 51–52.

CHAPTER III

DOMESTIC POLITICS AND THE MARCHAND MISSION, II: 1896–98

After the Ministry of Foreign Affairs granted approval for the Marchand mission, a delay occurred. In view of " all the fuss and bustle in November 1895," it seemed strange to everyone involved that Marchand did not depart for Africa immediately. Marchand's orders were not signed until 26 February 1896, almost four months after Berthelot gave his consent for the project.[1] Marchand later attributed this delay to bureaucratic inertia,[2] but it was in fact due to a high-level debate among the permanent officials at the Ministry of Colonies concerning the essence of the project.

Ernest Roume, director of the influential Bureau de l'Afrique, had cooperated fully with Marchand when the young captain first proposed his scheme. Marchand later wrote to him:

> . . . I have done nothing, *Monsieur le Directeur*, until now, without first seeking your advice or getting your approval—It was in your hands that I placed the report of 11 September 1895 on my proposal for the mission planned by order of the previous Minister of Colonies. It was directly from you that I got the invitation to go to the Minister of Foreign Affairs of the previous cabinet . . . When at the request of the Foreign Affairs department I handed in an additional analytic report (20 September 1895) specifying in detail the means and the final objective of the mission, it was to you that I went first of all to submit the wording, which you approved and I left with you a copy I had signed which you still have. It is on the basis of this latter document that the

1. Sanderson, p. 276.
2. Marchand, *Le Matin*, 24 June 1905.

Foreign Affairs Ministry, considering itself without doubt sufficiently enlightened, decided to give its full approval to the proposal for the mission by an official dispatch reproducing in part the wording of the analytic report.

Similar authority to proceed, the text of which must have been carefully weighed and signed by the Head of the [Colonial] Department himself, and coming after several months of study of the aforementioned proposal under two Cabinets, constitutes, I thought I could safely assume, a very reliable indication of support for this proposal—in the sense that from the point of view of broad foreign policy, the most serious of all, the risks of carrying it out are covered by the approval of French diplomacy whose intervention in this affair was directly provoked by the Colonial department— that is very probably by you, *Monsieur le Directeur*.[3]

In January Roume told an astonished Marchand that he had altered his view on the subject, however, and that the Marchand mission would have to be postponed or even abandoned. Nonetheless, within a month formal orders authorizing the Marchand mission were signed by Guieysse. During this time Roume remained adamantly opposed, and no pressure came from the Ministry of Foreign Affairs. Guieysse himself had earlier simply followed the advice of his senior political counsellor, Roume. Who intervened to reverse the decision of Roume and the Bureau de l'Afrique?

A clue to this mystery may be found in the inscriptions at the base of the stern bronze of Mangin which one passes when walking along avenue Duquesne en route to the colonial archives on rue Oudinot. Amid slogans which proclaim the military hero's credo —" *La plus grande France* " and " *Faire la guerre: c'est attaquer* " —are facts marking the first two steps of his career—" *Il était au Soudan* " and " *Il était à Fachoda avec Marchand.*" One might begin to wonder if these two experiences were in some way meaningfully linked together. Digging deeper, one learns that many of the most important officers of the Upper Nile projects began their careers in the Sudan. Monteil, Marchand, Mangin, Baratier, and Largeau all served under one man: Colonel Louis Archinard.[4]

3. MC, Afrique III, 32a, no. 5: Marchand to Roume, 26 January 1896. I have not attempted to correct Marchand's awkward grammar.

4. See J. Balteau *et al., Dictionnaire de biographie française* (Paris, 1933–59), for careers of these men.

Archinard is not as well-known as such famed French colonialists as de Brazza, Lyautey, and Gallieni, but in the minds of colonial enthusiasts he was one of the giants of French expansionism. In 1930, speaking before the Société de l'histoire des colonies, Lyautey proclaimed, "There are two names which between them dominate the history of our colonial development, Archinard and Gallieni . . ." [5] Archinard was made *commandant supérieur du Soudan français* in 1888, and by 1893, after four daring military campaigns, he had more than doubled the territory he had been sent to administer. The French Sudan was twenty million hectares in 1888, fifty million in 1893. Archinard had created, largely on his own initiative and on a shoestring budget, an empire equal in size to France itself.[6] During these campaigns, Marchand, Largeau, Baratier, and Mangin had received their first taste of empire-building, and had become imbued with Archinard's vision of "*la plus grande France.*"

Archinard did more than simply initiate the key figures of the Marchand mission into the experience of empire-building. In 1893 he left Africa and did not return, but he never abandoned his goal of further expanding the French Sudan. When he arrived in Paris, he established close links with the Comité de l'Afrique française [7] and quickly became one of the group's most influential and respected members. In the summer of 1895 he began to attend the regular meetings of the Comité's directors, and by 1900 Terrier could pay homage to him as a man "whom all of us colonialists hold in such high regard." [8] In 1894 Archinard became head of the Direction de la Défense at the Ministry of Colonies, and from this strategic position he collaborated with Marchand and the Comité in launching the Marchand mission.

In September the civilian Bureau de l'Afrique and the military Direction de la Défense had been in accord on the Marchand mission. But by the end of October there had occurred a division between the two groups on the strategy and tactics of the new project. By 31 October Archinard's department had completed

5. Général Edouard Réquin, *Archinard et le Soudan* (Paris, 1946), p. v.

6. *Ibid.*, p. 149. The Sudan's yearly budget reached a new high in 1893—a mere 634,000 francs. Also see MC, Mission 40: Campagne du Soudan (Archinard).

7. See BI, Fonds Terrier, 5938: Rapports du Colonel Louis Archinard (1890–1891). Dossier 5894 also contains correspondence between Archinard and Terrier.

8. BI, Fonds Terrier, 5904; Terrier to Marchand, 12 March 1900. *BCAF,* V (July 1895), 1; (August 1895), 1.

a " *projet d'instructions* " which embodied their scenario for the course of future events.[9]

Archinard's immediate concern was to eliminate Liotard, who had proved himself incapable of dealing with the African situation. A " military leader " with " military means " would play a " politico-military " role in the tradition of colonialism which Archinard had established while he was expanding the perimeters of the French Sudan. Liotard was to be ordered to " hand over to Captain Marchand the duties of the *commandant supérieur du Haut-Oubangui* " [10] and then return immediately to France. Because Marchand's loyalty was above all to his former commander, these orders would have left the Sudanese situation almost solely in the control of Archinard, a man to whom Marchand came to refer as " *mon maître.*" [11]

Roume quickly blocked this move, and the orders which embodied the views of the Directeur de la Défense at the Pavillon de Flore were never sent. In November, on the basis of a series of letters received from Liotard, the Bureau de l'Afrique drew up a long report entitled " Examen du projet de mission préparé par M. Marchand." [12] This report proposed a much less ambitious Upper Nile project that would replace Marchand with a civilian and would therefore be solidly under the control of the Direction Politique. The alternate mission envisioned an extension of French influence only as far as the Bahr-el-Homr, thus stopping short of Fashoda. There would be no alliance with the Mahdists, which Liotard believed was untenable; there would be no reopening of the Egyptian question, which Roume now considered too daring. The mission would be headed by the civilian Liotard, who had recently been promoted to *commissaire du gouvernement* for the Upper Ubangi. The report concluded by recommending that Liotard's strategy and tactics be approved and the Marchand mission abandoned. This study led Roume to withdraw his support for the Marchand mission.

Archinard, however, was not about to allow the civilians at the Pavillon de Flore to scuttle the Marchand mission.[13] He may well

9. MC, Afrique III, 32a, no. 4.
10. *Ibid.*
11. BI, Fonds Terrier, 5904; Marchand to Terrier, n. d.
12. MC, Afrique III, 32a, unnumbered.
13. On Archinard's strong support for the entire project, see MC, Afrique III, 32a, unnumbered: Extrait d'une lettre écrite au Général Archinard par M. le Capitaine Marchand, February 1897.

have reminded Guieysse that there was a great deal of support for the expedition at the Ministry of War. At any rate, the Ministry of War offered to supply the mission logistic support.[14] The arguments for and against the Marchand mission became more acrimonious. Roume's department began to refer to the Archinard-backed project as the "*mission du capitaine*"; Archinard reiterated his demand that Liotard be recalled.[15] By February 1896, therefore, there was a profound division between the two most powerful permanent officials at the Pavillon de Flore.

The Minister of Colonies, who had been so eager to accept the advice of his experts in October and November, was in a difficult position: his experts now disagreed among themselves. If either the Marchand or Liotard project had received the wholehearted and sustained support of the Minister of Colonies, if either had been executed without delay, then either might have succeeded. Instead, Guieysse avoided the responsibility of making the policy decision demanded by the division of opinion within his department. Unable to decide between the views of the highest authorities of the department, Guieysse delayed any final decision by approving parts of both projects: "Our role will indeed be particularly difficult," he wrote; "on the one hand we must not cease to maintain good relations with the Sultans [Liotard's view]; on the other, it is necessary to *ménager* the Mahdists and arrive on the Nile before Colonel Colville [Marchand's project.]."[16] Marchand was ordered to continue his mission, but it was to be under the supervision of Liotard; Liotard was given the power to order Marchand back to France if he saw fit.

The contradictions inherent in this approach are obvious, but Guieysse concluded on the note that, "thanks to their tact and ability," Marchand and Liotard would be able to find a solution to this "problem."[17] Thus, the Minister of Colonies avoided all responsibility by thrusting a series of extremely crucial policy decisions into the hands of a *commissaire* and a *capitaine*.

14. This may have been at the request of General Aristide-Emile-Anatole Baratier, the father of Marchand's colleague, Captain Baratier. See Balteau, *Dictionnaire de biographie française*, V, 195–99. General Baratier was head of the Direction des services administratives de l'armée in 1895. See also MC, Afrique III, 32a, no. 7.

15. MC, Afrique III, 32a, unnumbered: "Note: mission du capitaine," February 1896.

16. MC, Afrique III, 32a, no. 10: Guieysse to Berthelot, 24 February 1896.

17. *Ibid.*

II

In the summer of 1896 the Bourgeois cabinet was replaced by the Méline cabinet. Gabriel Hanotaux returned to the Ministry of Foreign Affairs, and the political scientist André Lebon became Minister of Colonies. The Méline government did not fall until the summer of 1898, and Hanotaux and Lebon benefited from this unusual ministerial stability by remaining at the Quai d'Orsay and the Pavillon de Flore for almost two full years. Despite their relatively long tenures of office, neither minister succeeded in imposing his will on the permanent officials at the colonial department by setting limits to the Marchand mission.

Soon after Hanotaux and Lebon took office, a new set of orders was issued which re-emphasized Marchand's subordination to the civilian Liotard.[18] There was nothing really new in this: it was simply a continuation of the Guieysse policy of giving Liotard responsibility for decisions that should have been made at the highest levels of the French government. Nevertheless, after the Fashoda crisis Hanotaux tried to absolve himself of responsibility for the debacle by claiming that he had inspired these new orders and that they had altered the entire nature of the mission. By placing a civilian in charge of the project, Hanotaux wrote, he had given the Marchand mission " an exclusively pacific character." [19] Although this may well have been the real intention of the new instructions, the means chosen were extremely ineffective.

Marchand was technically subordinate to Liotard, but the actual influence exerted by the civilian *commissaire* was dependent on the power wielded in the corridors of the Pavillon de Flore by his superior, Roume. As long as Roume and Liotard stood united against what they considered the " military recklessness " of the Direction de la Défense, there was the possibility that some pretext could be found to order Marchand back to Paris or, at the very least, to limit the means and goals of his mission. But toward the end of 1896 Liotard lost the most influential exponent of his " policy of moderation " when Roume ceased to be head of the Bureau de l'Afrique.

Roume was replaced by Gustave Binger, former governor-general of the Ivory Coast. Like so many people involved in the

18. *DDF*, XII, no. 411: Lebon to Liotard, 23 June 1896.
19. Hanotaux, *Le Partage d'Afrique: Fachoda* (Paris, 1909), pp. 108–9.

Marchand mission, Binger had served under Archinard in the Sudan before retiring to civilian life.[20] He was one of the earliest and most influential adherents of the Comité de l'Afrique française. His appointment to the highest permanent post in the civilian wing of the Ministry of Colonies was a striking victory for French expansionists, and probably reflected their growing influence.[21] The previous division between the Bureau de l'Afrique and the Direction de la Défense was ended, and the two departments now presented a united front on the tactics of the Marchand mission.

Without the support of Roume, Liotard's policy of moderation had little chance of survival. In fact, Liotard was now subordinate to Binger, and Binger was in full accord with Archinard. Thus, within a few months of the time when the Hanotaux-Lebon instructions had been sent to Liotard, they were rendered substantially ineffective.

If the Minister of Foreign Affairs had been willing to assert his full authority as a responsible minister, he could have substantially altered the nature of the Marchand mission by enforcing the restrictions which his predecessor had included in the letter approving the project. Berthelot had extended the approval of the Ministry of Foreign Affairs to a nonmilitary mission which " would not undertake an act of occupation; it would not even make political treaties [with native groups]." [22] Furthermore, the November approval did not extend to a reopening of the Egyptian question. Only with these reservations did Berthelot give his " entire adhesion " to the Marchand mission.

Hanotaux certainly knew that this was the only explicit written approval ever given the Marchand mission by the Ministry of Foreign Affairs, and if he had really been determined to give the mission an " exclusively pacific character," he could have cited this precedent and demanded compliance with it. But there is no evidence that Hanotaux ever followed such a course of action, and the permanent officials at the Pavillon de Flore simply swept aside the confused reservations of Berthelot. Thus, between the summer of 1896 and the fall of 1897, in the absence of any effective oppo-

20. Balteau, *Dictionnaire de biographie française*, VI.

21. BI, Fonds Terrier, 5891, no. 71: Binger to Alis, 6 December 1890; no. 72: 31 December 1890; no. 73: 12 January 1891; and other letters in 1892 and 1893. See also *BCAF*, I (January 1891), 1–2.

22. MC, Afrique III, 32a, Berthelot to Guieysse, 30 November 1895.

sition from the Quai d'Orsay, the Marchand mission emerged
as a full-blown expansionist military project under the complete
control of Archinard and Binger. The instructions which ordered
this transformation were issued by the Ministry of Colonies in
" flat defiance of Berthelot's directive and never communicated to,
much less approved by, the Quai d'Orsay." [23]

Marchand did everything which Berthelot had explicitly prohibited. He flew the Tricolor; he made treaties with the natives
of the Sudan; he occupied Fashoda; he styled himself " Commissaire du gouvernement français dans le haut Nil et le Bahr-el-
Ghazal." On reaching Fashoda, he hoisted the Tricolor over the
ancient fort and christened it " Fort St. Louis du Nil." And when
he refused to evacuate Fashoda after his encounter with the commander in chief of the Anglo-Egyptian army, his action produced
a major international crisis, even if it did not reopen the Egyptian
question in the manner which had been foreseen.

III

All of these events reflected a carefully planned scenario which
originated under the supervision of the Direction de la Défense.
The military planners of the Marchand mission scheduled the
project into four distinct phases.[24] During the first two phases the
project was known as " Mission B," and Marchand was instructed
to present his mission as an exploratory " expedition " charted for
peaceful and nonpolitical purposes. Once he was well into the
center of Africa, he was to wait for instructions which would allow
him to throw off the cloak of secrecy and style himself " Chef du
mission du Congo-nil." This would be phase three. In the fourth
phase he was to occupy Fashoda and annex the area which was to
be called " Afrique centrale française." The first two phases of
the Marchand mission lasted from the summer of 1896 to the fall
of 1897. The last two unfolded between November 1897 and
October 1898. Thus, until the fall of 1897 the Marchand mission
resembled a peaceful exploratory expedition, but after that date
the real intentions of the mission emerged.

After the Marchand mission was en route to Fashoda, its backers

---

23. Sanderson, p. 276.
24. MC, Missions 42–43. These dossiers give full details because they are in
the archives of the Direction de la Défense, and not in the civilian Afrique III
series.

at the Pavillon de Flore decided that an auxiliary support mission should be launched from eastern Africa. In early 1897 the first such mission, headed by Clochette, left Ethiopia bound for Fashoda.[25] There is no evidence to indicate that the Ministry of Foreign Affairs was ever informed of this initiative.

In March, however, Lebon considered Hanotaux's approval necessary for yet another new departure in Upper Nile policy: an effort was now made to launch a joint French-Ethiopian mission toward Fashoda. Lebon pressed Hanotaux to approve the new venture, but was met with strong resistance. Lebon therefore resorted to tactics employed earlier by Delcassé in obtaining approval for the Monteil mission. On 11 March Hanotaux was overruled by a majority of the Méline cabinet, just as he had been outvoted three years earlier in the Dupuy cabinet.[26] On 14 March Lebon wrote Lagarde, the representative of the colonial department in Addis Ababa, that a joint French-Ethiopian advance toward Fashoda was now absolutely " indispensable " for the success of the Upper Nile project.[27] Lagarde soon completed negotiations with the Negus Menelik. In return for a French agreement to partition the Nile Valley with Ethiopia, Menelik gave his support for a mission to reinforce Marchand at Fashoda.[28] By the fall of 1897 a Convention pour le Nil blanc had been signed. In addition, a mission under the command of Marquis de Bonchamps and an Ethiopian mission which followed him closely were en route to link up with Marchand.[29]

By November 1897 Marchand had reached Fort Hossinger. In October he had received a message which he entered in his journal

25. Sanderson, p. 295.
26. *DDF*, XIII, no. 137: Lebon to Hanotaux, 5 March 1897, footnote, minute by Nisard recording the opinion of Hanotaux; and no. 149: Lebon to Lagarde, 14 March 1897, footnote, minute recording cabinet decision. See also Sanderson, pp. 293–95. For a more detailed discussion of this important cabinet decision, see below, p. 137.
27. *DDF*, XIII, no. 149: Lebon to Lagarde, 14 March 1897.
28. *DDF*, XIII, no. 159: Convention pour le Nil blanc, 20 March 1897. For a complete account see Sanderson, " Contributions from African Sources to the History of European Competition in the Upper Valley of the Nile," *JAH*, III (1962), 69–90; and Sanderson, " The Foreign Policy of Negus Menelik, 1896–1898," *JAH*, V (1964), 87–97. All other references to Sanderson are to his book, rather than these articles.
29. Charles Michel, *Mission de Bonchamps: vers Fachoda à la rencontre de la mission Marchand* (Paris, 1900), pp. 250–53; and Langer, *Diplomacy of Imperialism*, pp. 540–46.

as " lettre officielle No. 126." " Request Liotard by the quickest means," the letter read, " to activate Marchand toward the Nile to link up with Clochette who continues to advance toward Fashoda." [30] Marchand's response was: " Very important order to advance, coming from the Government. I have received a letter from the *haut protecteur* of the mission. Finally! Occupation of Fashoda decided by France." [31] This was the signal for which Marchand had been waiting. Now he could be free of the restrictions of " Mission B " and enter phase three of his mission. Marchand wrote Liotard that he was elated that the " careful methods which [he had] employed up to the present " could now be abandoned, and added gravely, " I am assuming the role of head of mission with all the risks which that entails." Everything, Marchand concluded, must now be subordinated " to the obligation, that you point out to me by order of the [Colonial] Department, of reaching Fashoda as quickly as possible. I will get there, regardless of the costs." All previous letters to Liotard had been headed " Mission B " and signed simply " Marchand." This letter was headed " Phase Three " and signed " Le Captaine Marchand chef de la mission Congo-Nil." [32]

In the fall of 1897 the Upper Nile project for which French colonialists had worked since 1893 seemed close to success. The Minister of Colonies had accepted the tactics of Marchand and Archinard, and the reservations of moderates in the French government had all been swept aside. Marchand was within a few months of reaching Fashoda. Ethiopian cooperation had been obtained for a flanking operation from the east which had received the approval of the Méline cabinet.[33] The Minister of Foreign Affairs' efforts to restrict the scope of the project by making it " exclusively pacific " had failed completely. The Comité, Archinard, Binger, and Marchand could see the completion of their project in sight. Things had gone well for this group of determined men.[34]

30. MC, Afrique III, 32a, unnumbered (near no. 41).
31. Cited in Delebecque, *Vie du Général Marchand*, pp. 109–10. Who was the " *haut protecteur* " of the Marchand mission? Sanderson presumes that he was Lebon, but this seems unlikely because Marchand almost certainly would have referred to him as M. le Ministre, as was his practice. It was probably Archinard.
32. MC, Afrique III, 32a, no. 41: Marchand to Liotard, 3 November 1897.
33. *Ibid.*
34. For a discussion of the more general factors which made success possible for these men, see below, pp. 138–39.

IV

Another group of equally determined men had not had such success. Mathieu Dreyfus, the brother of Captain Alfred Dreyfus, had never accepted the verdict of the military court-martial of 1894 and had worked since that date to collect evidence that would free his brother. He had been successful in discovering a great number of facts indicating Dreyfus' innocence, but he had little success in bringing this new evidence before a wide public. In the fall of 1897, however, Mathieu Dreyfus had the good fortune to obtain the sympathetic understanding of an influential French parliamentarian, Auguste Scheurer-Kestner.

In November 1897 rumors reached the Quai d'Orsay to the effect that Scheurer-Kestner planned a plea in the French Senate for a reconsideration of the Dreyfus case. Hanotaux quickly arranged to meet with the senator to discuss the case. The Minister of Foreign Affairs admitted that it was certainly Scheurer-Kestner's right to believe in the innocence of Dreyfus, but argued that a man of responsibility should not compromise " the national interest " by a public campaign on behalf of Dreyfus. There would certainly be " complications of a diplomatic order " if the Dreyfus affair were pushed to the forefront of public opinion, concluded Hanotaux, and this would be most unfortunate for France.[35]

When Hanotaux first heard of the Dreyfus case, he had opposed indictment because he feared dangerous " international consequences "; now he opposed the reopening of the case for precisely the same reasons. The events of the following year were to demonstrate only too clearly the accuracy of Hanotaux's forecast. By a strange twist of events, the destinies of Captain Jean-Baptiste Marchand and Captain Alfred Dreyfus became momentarily linked between January and November of 1898.

35. MAE, Papiers Hanotaux, II, " Ma conversation avec M. Scheurer-Kestner," 6 November 1897.

PART II

DOMESTIC POLITICS AND THE CONDUCT
OF FOREIGN POLICY

CHAPTER IV

THE INTERNATIONAL DIMENSION OF THE DREYFUS AFFAIR, JANUARY–MARCH 1898

During the first week of January 1898 the French Minister of Foreign Affairs received a confidential letter from a political informant living in Paris. Within a few days, the letter warned, a " *bombe politique* " would be exploded which would shake the very foundations of the French political world.[1] The explosion came in the form of Emile Zola's letter entitled " J'accuse " which was published on 13 January in *L'Aurore*. Zola's reopening of the Dreyfus case had far-reaching political consequences, both domestic and international.

" J'accuse " marked a new stage in the history of the Dreyfus affair.[2] Between 1895 and the last part of 1897, there had been no dramatic developments in the case. But behind the scenes enough evidence had accumulated to convince Mathieu Dreyfus and other Dreyfusards that a certain Commandant Esterhazy was the real author of the bordereau, the key piece of evidence that had led to the conviction of Dreyfus. On 16 November 1897, Scheurer-Kestner, in defiance of Hanotaux's request, made public a letter to the Minister of War containing the charges against the new suspect. In order to quickly end this speculation, the Méline government and the Ministry of War decided to bring Esterhazy before a court-martial, and on 11 January he was duly acquitted of the charges against him. This event led directly to Emile Zola's open letter of protest to the President of the Republic.

Before 1898 the Dreyfusards had argued that a juridical error had been committed and that it should be set right. Zola now

1. I have not been able to examine this document personally. It is in volume X of the Papiers Hanotaux, which, at the time I was in Paris, was not yet available to scholars. Its contents were described to me in some detail by M. Georges Dethan, head of the archives of the Ministry of Foreign Affairs.
2. Chastenet, *Histoire de la Troisième République*, pp. 116–17.

implied much more. Not only had an error been committed, he argued, but highly placed officers in the French army had conspired to keep the case from being revised. In general, the Dreyfusards had worked quietly for revision of the case; Zola rejected their methods: his letter was in no way restrained but was rather a violent and emotional polemic. Its tone is well demonstrated in these concluding paragraphs:

> I accuse General Billot of having had in his hands certain proofs of Dreyfus' innocence and at having suppressed them, of being guilty of the crime of betraying society and justice for a political objective and to save the compromised General Staff . . . .
>
> . . . .
>
> I accuse the War offices of having led an abominable press campaign, especially in the *Eclair* and in the *Echo de Paris*, to mislead public opinion and to conceal their blunder.
>
> I accuse, finally, the first Court-Martial of having broken the law in condemning the accused on secret evidence, and I accuse the second Court-Martial of having concealed this illegality, on orders, and committing in turn the juridical crime of knowingly acquitting a guilty man.
>
> . . . .
>
> As for the people whom I have accused, I do not know them; I have never seen them, I bear them no hatred or bitterness. They are only entities to me, examples of social malfeasance. And the act that I have accomplished here is only a revolutionary means to hasten the revelation of truth and justice.[3]

The " revolutionary means " which Zola employed certainly succeeded in dramatically placing the issues of the Dreyfus affair before the public. *L'Aurore*, in response to public demand, published a record 300,000 copies of its special edition which contained " J'accuse." [4] Political activity associated with the Dreyfus affair increased immediately. In January and February 1898, over 27,000 Parisians attended demonstrations or public meetings where

3. *L'Aurore*, 13 January 1898.
4. Johnson, *France and the Dreyfus Affair*, p. 119.

the Dreyfus affair was a central topic of discussion.[5] This wave of interest soon began to subside, however, and by the time of the parliamentary elections of May 1898 the Dreyfus affair had become a peripheral issue.[6] A retrospective study of these elections, based on extensive police records, concluded:

> The overwhelming majority of opinion was forcefully against revision, and the political parties accommodated their views to those of their electorate. The groups which would later massively adhere to the cause of revision then showed only prudence and reserve . . . . Almost no candidate or party proclaimed in favor of Dreyfus, and the party committees in addition required, as a minimum, silence on the question . . . .[7]

Therefore, Zola seems to have failed in his attempt to initiate an irresistible current of opinion in favor of revision. Nevertheless, by conditioning the French public to the facts of the Dreyfus affair, by injecting an element of passion into these events, and by charging the upper echelons of the French military establishment with conspiracy, Zola's letter marked a decisive turning point in the domestic history of the affair.

II

" J'accuse " was also a turning point in the international dimension of the Dreyfus affair. At its inception the diplomatic repercussions of the case were limited to Franco-German relations.[8] The first diplomatic incident came within a month of the night that Hanotaux warned Mercier of the " international difficulties " which would result if the Dreyfus case were pursued. The origin of these difficulties, Hanotaux told Mercier, would be exaggerated press accounts. The Minister of Foreign Affairs warned, " You

5. Archives du Préfecture de Police (APP), Ba/104: Rapport quotidien, January–March 1898.

6. APP, Ba/105: Rapport quotidien, April–August 1898.

7. APP, Ba/653: Elections législatives de 1898, " Situation générale des partis politiques en 1898," a report prepared by Renseignements généraux soon after the events. Also see Johnson, *France and the Dreyfus Affair*, pp. 130–34.

8. Maurice Baumont, *Aux sources de l'affaire; l'affaire Dreyfus d'après les archives diplomatiques* (Paris, 1959), p. 49. " *L'Affaire Dreyfus*," writes Baumont, " *est fondamentalement une affaire franco-allemande.*" This, as we shall see, is a correct description of the period down to 1898.

can imagine the polemics! " [9] They were not long in coming. The press of the right, which took its lead from the anti-Semitic *La Libre Parole*, played on popular fears of Germany by underlining the role of the German embassy in the affair.[10] This provoked the German ambassador, Count Münster, to demand an official denial of German complicity in the case. In the end, not one, but a series of French denials were published to please the Germans, and periodically between 1895 and 1897 there recurred similar diplomatic incidents.[11]

The Quai d'Orsay also had to deal with problems raised by Dreyfusard activity abroad. As early as 1896 Dreyfusard writers had begun a campaign to rally foreign opinion to the revisionist cause, but they had had almost no success. In November 1897 an uneasy silence still reigned abroad on the subject. On 6 November the Quai d'Orsay received a long memorandum from the embassy in Berlin entitled " Au Sujet de l'affaire Dreyfus." The French ambassador to Germany, Marquis de Noailles, observed that the revisionist campaign had had almost no impact in Germany.[12] The Quai d'Orsay probably concluded, on the basis of the trickle of reports reaching France from the other countries of the world, that the situation in Germany was a reflection of the lack of revisionist sympathy in the world as a whole.[13]

" J'accuse " shattered the universal silence and initiated a cacophony of international protest. Hundreds of congratulatory telegrams poured into Paris from all over the world: from Berlin, Vienna, and Rome; from St. Petersburg, Warsaw, and Budapest; from London, New York, Washington, and Amsterdam they came—all in praise of Zola, all in favor of revising the Dreyfus

---

9. Paléologue, *Journal de l'affaire Dreyfus*, p. 4.

10. For a complete account see P. Boussel, *L'Affaire Dreyfus et la presse* (Paris, 1960).

11. See MAE, Papiers Hanotaux, IX: " Affaire Dreyfus: incident Münster," January 1898. Another account of the " Münster incident" may be found in the testimony given by Casimir-Périer before the Cour de cassation, AN, 53AP: Papiers de Sallintin.

12. MAE, Allemagne, NS53: Relations avec la France, Affaire Dreyfus, no. 6: Berlin to Paris, 6 November 1897. Almost all of the correspondence on the affair is collected in the Allemagne dossiers, NS53–NS59, hereafter cited as Affaire Dreyfus.

13. Only 89 pages of correspondence on the affair reached the Quai d'Orsay between 7 September 1896 and 12 January 1898; by contrast there were 639 pages in the first month and a half after the Zola letter. See MAE, NS53–54: Affaire Dreyfus.

case, all sharply critical of the French army. Zola had tapped a rich reservoir of humanitarian feeling in Europe and the world. He was for many a " defender of civilization," the " courageous advocate of truth and the irrepressible champion of right and justice." For others Zola was " a great genius, a noble heart," who sustained a struggle for justice which " honored humanity." This was the tone of the mass of telegrams which were carefully collected and analyzed by the French Ministry of Foreign Affairs, and which signaled a rising tide of world opinion in favor of revision.[14]

So strong was the revisionist movement in Germany and Italy that the governments of these two countries were soon involved. In response to a question posed by a member of the Reichstag, Secretary of State Bülow made the following declaration on 24 January:

> You can understand that I approach the question only with the utmost care. To act otherwise could be considered an intervention on our part in the internal affairs of France.
>
> I will limit myself to saying in a most categorical manner that absolutely no German agent has ever had relations or links of any kind with the French ex-Captain Dreyfus who is presently imprisoned on Devil's Island.[15]

This was quickly followed by a similar declaration in the Italian Chamber on 1 February:

> We can affirm in a most explicit manner that neither our military attaché nor any other agent or representative of the Italian government has ever had any relationship, direct or indirect, with ex-Captain Dreyfus.[16]

These government declarations only confirmed to Germans and Italians that Dreyfus was innocent, since it was now generally known that he had been charged with having given secrets to the German military attaché, a man who was reportedly in collusion

14. MAE, NS53: Affaire Dreyfus, nos. 96–110, 115–32, 139–61, 164–73, 175–201, 219–36, 321–38, 344–63, and 379–99 are the major collections of telegrams at the Quai d'Orsay. In an article inspired by the retired Bismarck, the Germans who sent such telegrams were reprimanded for intervening in the domestic affairs of other countries. See NS54, no. 332: Berlin to Paris, 14 February 1898.

15. Baumont, *Aux sources de l'affaire*, p. 194.

16. *Ibid.*, pp. 197–98.

with the Italian military attaché. Revisionist sentiment continued to soar.[17]

The world revisionist movement quickly became a matter of concern to the French diplomatic corps. In contrast to the situation which he had described in November 1897, the Marquis de Noailles now reported that Germany was alive with talk of the affair, and that the press was now almost solidly in favor of revision.[18] A similar shift was noted in the other nations of the Triple Alliance. From Rome the French ambassador wrote that there had been little concern with the affair prior to 13 January 1898, but that " after the publication of Emile Zola's recent letter to the President of the Republic, a general outburst occurred." [19] The French ambassador in Vienna reported that Austrian opinion, even " society itself," was " anti-French " and pro-Dreyfusard. He concluded on the alarming note that if the Dreyfus affair were prolonged it could not fail " to compromise the position that France occupies among the first ranks of the European Powers." [20]

French concern with the world revisionist movement was not limited to the countries allied against France in the Triple Alliance. There were even difficulties in Russia, a country with close ties to France. In areas of Russia where there were large Jewish ghettos, the St. Petersburg embassy reported, pro-Dreyfusard sentiment was running high, and aggravated an already tense situation. Zola was being praised as a great man among Russian intellectuals who looked to the West for inspiration. Although there was little Dreyfusard sympathy in Russian government circles, there was at the Czarist court some apprehension concerning the reliability of France as an ally.[21]

From Great Britain the French ambassador reported that the

17. For a complete account of the Italian response to the affair, see Baumont, " L'Affaire Dreyfus et l'opinion italienne d'après les archives diplomatiques," *Rassegna storica del Resorgimento*, IX (1964), pp. 345–50.

18. MAE, Allemagne, NS60: Relations avec l'Angleterre, 1897–1914, no. 16: Berlin to Paris, 23 January 1898.

19. MAE, NS53: Affaire Dreyfus, no. 287: Rome to Paris, 20 January 1898.

20. *Ibid.*, no. 91: Vienna to Paris, 13 January 1898.

21. MAE, Russie, NS1: Politique intérieure, dossier générale, St. Petersburg to Paris, 29 January 1898. And NS57: Affaire Dreyfus, Consulate (Odessa) to Paris, 20 August 1898. Russian support prompted an anonymous French revisionist to publish a short pamphlet entitled *La Russie et l'affaire Dreyfus* (Paris, 1898). On the " Westernizers " in the Russian intelligensia, see Hugh Seton-Watson, *The Decline of Imperial Russia, 1855–1914* (New York, 1961), pp. 22–23.

affair was harming still further the already strained relationship between France and Great Britain. "[Public] opinion," wrote Baron Courcel, "is almost unanimous in proclaiming that Dreyfus has been illegally condemned, and it is consequently disposed to accept the most injurious judgments on the vices of the administration of justice in France, and on the dangers of the development of a militarist spirit . . . ."[22] There were similar messages from the less powerful states of Europe, ranging from Spain in the south to Denmark in the north.[23] In addition, the Quai d'Orsay received reports of revisionist activities in areas as removed from France as Australia, South America, and the United States.[24]

In January 1898, therefore, very largely as a result of the publication of "J'accuse," the Dreyfus affair ceased to be a purely Franco-German issue. It broadened to affect French relations with all of the European powers and, to a lesser extent, with most other countries in the world. Although the world revisionist movement alarmed French diplomats throughout Europe, it was in the end to have its most far-reaching consequences in the realm of Franco-British relations.

III

Sir Edmund Monson, the British ambassador in Paris, was deeply concerned with the Dreyfus question. Monson's task was to observe carefully the changing domestic situation within France, and report to the Foreign Office at Whitehall the potential effect of the affair on French attitudes and policies toward Great Britain and the other powers of Europe.

Prior to January 1898 Monson had known no more of the Drey-

22. MAE, Grande Bretagne, NS 11: Relations avec la France, 1897–1898, no. 208: London to Paris, 9 February 1898.

23. MAE, NS53: Affaire Dreyfus, no. 240: Denmark to Paris, 19 January 1898; no. 263: Madrid to Paris, 20 January 1898; no. 304: Amsterdam to Paris, 21 January 1898; no. 306: Brussels to Paris, 21 January 1898.

24. See the numerous reports in NS53 and NS54, Affaire Dreyfus. For a more detailed account of these reports see Baumont, "L'Affaire Dreyfus dans la diplomatie française," in *Studies in Diplomatic History and Historiography in Honour of G. P. Gooch*, ed. A. O. Sarkissian (London, 1961), pp. 26–47. On attitudes in the United States over the affair, see Rose A. Halperin, "The American Reaction to the Dreyfus Affair" (Master's thesis, Columbia University, 1941). More monographs like Halperin's, dealing in detail with each of the European countries, would be of great value. Taken together, they might reveal a great deal about European politics at the close of the nineteenth century and offer a rich source for studies in comparative history. The French response to the world movement, rather than the nuances of the movement itself, is, of course, the theme of the present chapter.

fus case than what he learned from the newspapers. Another member of the embassy staff, military attaché Colonel Douglas Dawson, was much better informed. Dawson, the son of Lord Cremaine, had previously been attaché in Vienna. In 1895 he was promoted and given the prized post in Paris. Dawson later wrote in his memoirs that within a year he was "unwittingly and most unwillingly drawn into the vortex of the Dreyfus case . . . ." [25] This involvement was the direct result of Dawson's frequent contact with other foreign military attachés stationed in Paris. These men, in the course of their duties, often became well-acquainted with one another.[26]

By May 1896 Dawson was on friendly terms with both the German and Italian military attachés, Colonels Schwartzkoppen and Panizzardi. Toward the end of 1897, at Dawson's avenue du Bois garden apartment, Panizzardi told Dawson that Schwartzkoppen was certain that Esterhazy and not Dreyfus was the author of the bordereau. Dawson snapped: "Do you mean to tell me that that poor man, eating his heart out and grilling on that island, is innocent, and our colleague knew it? If so, you can tell him I never wish to speak to him again." [27] But Dawson's quick anger was soon quieted when Schwartzkoppen came to him and explained that he had always believed that Dreyfus had been convicted on evidence other than the bordereau. Schwartzkoppen then confided to his friend that he was confused and unable to decide exactly what to do, since it now appeared that the bordereau was the key to the case against Dreyfus. Dawson advised him to confess all he knew to the head of the German mission in Paris and then depart France "before the storm burst." [28]

Dawson presented a special "secret report" to Monson on 13 January 1898, the very day the "storm" of the affair broke. Monson then consulted the German ambassador, Count Münster, and was told that Dreyfus had never had any dealings with any staff member of the German embassy. Monson then asked about Esterhazy. "Ah, the other gentleman," Münster replied, "we know him well." [29] The following day Dawson submitted another secret

25. Dawson, *Soldier-Diplomat*, p. 220.
26. See Alfred Vagts, *The Military Attaché* (Princeton, 1967), for a discussion of the role of the attaché.
27. Dawson, *Soldier-Diplomat*, p. 221.
28. *Ibid.*
29. PRO, FO 27/3393, no. 19: Monson to Salisbury, 14 January 1898 (enclosing Dawson's secret report).

report which argued not only that Dreyfus was innocent but also that his continued imprisonment was the result of a conspiracy of highly placed generals in the French army.[30] Monson reported this conspiracy theory to Whitehall without comment in January, but in the coming months, as he became more and more disillusioned with the behavior of the French General Staff, he was increasingly disposed to accept the possibility of conspiracy in the French army. This disposition came to play an even greater role in the fall of 1898 when the Dreyfus affair and Anglo-French relations simultaneously took a grave turn in the direction of severe crisis.[31]

In January and February 1898, in Monson's view, events had not reached the crisis stage. "The demonstrations in Paris," he reported to the Foreign Office, " are almost entirely confined to the students of the Quartier Latin, who behaved very much as the undergraduates of an English university would do on the occasion of a Town and Gown row." He was, however, concerned " with the effect which the sensitiveness of the public and the irritation of the Army might have on . . . international relations." [32]

This concern was shared by Monson's colleagues who headed the elegant array of foreign embassies in Paris. In the era of the Old Diplomacy, Paris was considered to be the most illustrious assignment in the diplomatic world, the pinnacle of success in a diplomatic career.[33] The men chosen to represent the Great Powers in Paris were the elder statesmen of their profession. Sir Edmund John Monson was typical of this group. He was born in Chart Lodge, Kent, in 1835, the second son of William John Sixth Lord Monson. The family had received its noble title in the sixteenth century when William Monson distinguished himself in battle against the Spanish Armada. Monson had begun his diplomatic career as a clerk in the Foreign Office in 1856. As a reward for forty years of distinguished service at various capitals of Europe, he was appointed ambassador to Paris in 1896.[34] This made him

30. *Ibid.*, no. 24: Monson to Salisbury, 16 January 1898 (enclosing Dawson's subsequent secret report).

31. See below, pp. 110–12.

32. PRO, FO 27/3393, no. 31: Monson to Salisbury, 21 January 1898.

33. The British press, which accepted the judgment of the Foreign Office, often spoke of the Paris embassy as " the most distinguished and important place in the whole foreign service of the British Empire." MAE, Grande Bretagne, NS8: dossier générale, no. 346: (press annex), 12 November 1898.

34. Leonard C. Wood, " Sir Edmund Monson, Ambassador to France," (Ph. D.

a relative newcomer in the diplomatic society of Paris. Count
Georges de Münster, whose father had won the hereditary title
of Landmarschall of Hanover for his bravery in the Napoleonic
wars, had been the German ambassador to France since 1885.[35]
Count Giuseppe Tornielli-Brussati di Vergano had come to Paris
in 1895 after a brilliant career to head the Italian embassy.[36]

Monson was on especially good terms with Münster and Tornielli, and because of the unique roles of Germany and Italy in
the Dreyfus affair, he naturally turned to them for their views on
its possible effects on French policy. Their attitude was strongly
shaped by their social backgrounds and their ages: Münster was
born in 1839, and Tornielli in 1836. Both their fathers had fought
in the Napoleonic wars; they had childhood memories of the revo-
lutions of 1848 and had been adults at the time of the Commune.
Thus, they were conditioned by their own historical experience to
view France as intrinsically unstable; and, in the tradition of
Metternich, they inevitably saw in domestic instability a prelude
to European instability and general war. By the middle of February
both the German and Italian ambassadors were trying to persuade
Monson that the Dreyfus affair had produced in France a movement similar to Boulangism, and that this violent and growing
nationalism of the right would soon destroy the peace of Europe.

In the guarded style of his official correspondence, Monson
reported the views of his colleagues to Whitehall. According to
the Germans and Italians, Monson wrote, " [France is fast be-
coming] a standing danger and menace to Europe: . . . her relations with other countries are becoming abnormal; . . . she is
recurring to the frame of mind of one hundred years ago, when
she looked upon the rest of Europe as banded against her, and
when she had but the one thought, with which she is now possessed, that between herself and destruction there stands only her
army." The British ambassador added that many other intelligent
observers " are losing all hope that France can much longer escape
an internal convulsion; a convulsion in which the army will take a
prominent part, and which will equally be followed by a foreign
war." [37]

thesis, University of Pennsylvania, 1960), pp. 1–14. It was rumored that Monson
had been chosen over Lord Lansdown for the Paris embassy.
    35. An excellent profile of Münster is given in Baumont, *Aux sources de l'affaire*,
pp. 49–56.
    36. *Ibid.*, pp. 171–72.
    37. PRO, FO 27/3393, no. 109: Monson to Salisbury, 26 February 1898.

Monson, however, was very far from sounding an urgent warning. He labeled the alarm signals of his ambassadorial colleagues " gloomy forebodings," and reported them only as " conjectures for what they are worth . . . . " [38] In a private letter of 21 January to Lord Salisbury, however, Monson wrote quite openly of " the susceptibility of the French warrior, who in view of all these supposed attacks upon his honour may be inspired with the idea of vindicating at the expense of perfidious Albion . . . . " [39] Whether or not this " disquieting possibility " would become a reality depended, according to Monson, on the future course of domestic politics in France. On this question Monson offered the following observation:

> People of various stations of life and of various political complexions seem to be disturbed at the turn events are taking in France in connection with the Dreyfus case. But it appears to me that we are still very far off from the moment when Paris will descend into the streets, and start a fresh revolution; although when one sees how very little ballast the vessel of State really carries, one cannot help feeling that she would labour terribly even in a moderate gale; while a sudden squall might capsize her altogether.[40]

It was Monson's opinion that the events provoked by Zola were only a moderate gale; a much more violent storm would have to descend on France before the sceptical and cautious British ambassador would become convinced of the " gloomy forebodings " which had begun to spread throughout Europe in January and February 1898. Monson's " sudden squall " did not come until six months after the publication of " J'accuse." [41]

IV

Hanotaux, like Monson, was deeply concerned with the impact of the Dreyfus affair on Franco-British relations.[42] This was not because the British had played a special role in the espionage

38. *Ibid.*
39. CCO, Salisbury Papers, A/116: France (from), 1895–1900. no. 2: Monson to Salisbury, 21 January 1898.
40. *Ibid.*
41. See below, pp. 110–13.
42. MAE, Grande Bretagne, NS11: Relations avec la France, Hanotaux to Courcel, 1 February 1898.

dimension of the affair similar to that of Germany and Italy, but rather because Franco-British relations were already strained as a result of their competition for several areas in Africa. Hanotaux believed that the affair was complicating an already difficult situation. He resolved, therefore, to intervene personally.[43]

On 26 January Hanotaux summoned the British ambassador to the Quai d'Orsay to discuss the Dreyfus affair and Franco-British relations. The French Foreign Minister complained to Monson that the British press, by attacking the French government for its policy toward the Dreyfus case, was intervening in " what is purely a French domestic question." Hanotaux told Monson that any alteration of the "*chose jugée*" would "plunge France into anarchy." Monson countered by saying that in a free society there was little the British government could do to prevent press accounts of the affair. This clearly did not satisfy Hanotaux, and led directly to a hardening of his attitude toward Great Britain.[44]

Only a few days after his encounter with Monson, Hanotaux sent an urgent cable to Baron Courcel in London. In it he expressed his belief that many European diplomats, including the British, were convinced that the Dreyfus affair was weakening France.[45] A primary goal of French diplomacy, he suggested, should be to convince these diplomats that France was strong in spite of the affair. More specifically, he ordered Baron Courcel not to make any concessions in the protracted Franco-British negotiations dealing with a delimitation of borders in disputed territory along the Niger in West Africa. He concluded on the following emotional note:

> They perhaps believe that we are being weakened by the Dreyfus Affair. But they are wrong. They see us only through the eyes of the Jewish press. The country is holding well [under the strain], and, more importantly, its interests will be defended as energetically as ever.[46]

---

43. *Ibid.*, note du ministre: Sir Edmund Monson, 24 January 1898.
44. *Ibid.*
45. Hanotaux seems to have been unaware that many diplomats believed that the affair, rather than weakening France, was in fact making her more belligerent.
46. *Ibid.*, Hanotaux to Monson, 1 February 1898.

CHAPTER V

PRELUDE TO CRISIS, MARCH–AUGUST 1898

During the first months of 1898, Hanotaux reaffirmed even more energetically than before his determination to defend French interests on the Upper Nile. On 23 January, *Le Temps*, probably at the request of the Quai d'Orsay, published an article which stated in the most dogmatic terms the " absolute right " of France to territory in the Nile Valley.[1] This prepared the way for Hanotaux's February statement in the Chamber:

> I will say only one word on the Egyptian question. As M. Deloncle himself has rightly stated, no one speaks of this question, but everyone thinks of it. . . . our thought is fixed on this question as on all those that relate to French interests. We will defend the rights of Egypt . . . [and] . . . the destinies of the Nile basin and continental Africa.[2]

Like most of Hanotaux's speeches, this one was highly abstract. Nevertheless, with its emphasis on both the defense of the " rights " of Egypt and the " destinies of the Nile basin," Hanotaux seemed to be conditioning French public opinion for an approaching confrontation with Great Britain in the Egyptian Sudan.

In Great Britain also there was renewed interest in the question of the Upper Nile. Although the existence of the Marchand mission was public knowledge in Britain, the final goal of the expedition was a matter of speculation. There were, reported chief French political adviser Geoffray from the embassy in London, two interpretations of the French advance toward the Upper Nile.[3] On the one hand, there were those who believed that Marchand

1. PRO, FO 27/3393, no. 38: Monson to Salisbury, 23 January 1898.
2. *Journal officiel*, 7 February 1898.
3. Geoffray's formal title was *Conseiller d'embassade*.

was the head of a semiprivate and nonpolitical " exploring party ";
others suspected—quite correctly—that this " exploring party "
was a mere façade. The latter group argued, recalling the Grey
Declaration of 1895, that Marchand's presence at Fashoda should
be viewed by Britain as a decidedly " unfriendly act." [4] During the
first months of 1898, however, the public remained uncertain
about the true character of the Marchand mission.

II

An official debate on the actual intentions of the Marchand mission had been going on within the British government since 1896.[5]
During the entire course of this discussion, Sir John Charles
Ardagh, Director of British Military Intelligence, played a prominent role. On the basis of clandestine intelligence, Ardagh had
argued as early as November 1896 that Marchand, with the help
of the Emperor Menelik, would soon be solidly entrenched in the
Egyptian Sudan, and that the area was to be partitioned between
France and Ethiopia.[6]

In the summer of 1897 Ardagh's argument gained new support
when the Foreign Office received news that numerous French-
inspired missions had departed from Addis Ababa in the direction
of Fashoda. The Directorate of Military Intelligence favored immediate countermeasures, but reminded the Foreign Office that the
combined strength of French-controlled missions and the Mahdists,
who stood between Cairo and Fashoda as a kind of buffer state,
presented a formidable military obstacle. Ardagh was convinced
that the Egyptian army was not " strong enough to undertake the
enterprise " of re-establishing control in the Sudan without support, and added that the " possible demands upon the British Army
in the world at large leave but little margin for furnishing such
a force." [7] Despite this pessimistic estimate, Ardagh concluded
by arguing that Britain should mount a substantial effort in the
Nile or resign itself to a French takeover.

Lord Salisbury, a Conservative and a cautious Prime Minister

4. MAE, Egypte, NS30: Campagne du Soudan, no. 26: Geoffray to Hanotaux,
12 January 1898.

5. PRO, FO 27/3301, Cowston to Foreign Office, 16 June and 12 August 1896.
Cited by Sanderson, p. 254.

6. *Ibid.*, Ardagh to Foreign Office, 6 November 1896; and FO 27/3368, same
to same, 9 February 1897. Cited by Sanderson, p. 255.

7. PRO 30/40: Ardagh Papers, Memoranda, I, no. 29, 23 July 1897.

who also headed the Foreign Office, accepted the logic of the situation. Toward the end of 1897 he made the final decision to detail British troops to the Egyptian army, a force already under the command of Sir Herbert Kitchener.[8] On 26 January 1898 the Salisbury cabinet authorized Kitchener to advance to Khartoum.[9] Soon after this decision Salisbury gravely remarked that " within six months we will be at war with France." [10]

III

Hanotaux followed the British military buildup in Egypt with intense interest.[11] The new element in the situation, according to reports reaching Paris from London, was the introduction of British troops alongside the Egyptian army.[12] During the first half of January British battalions began arriving in Cairo, and by 1 February there were 3,000 British troops in Egypt. In addition, 14,000 of the Egyptian army's 25,000 troops had been placed under Kitchener's command.[13] This impressive show of force had a disquieting effect at the Quai d'Orsay.[14]

Also disquieting was the intelligence report submitted to the Ministry of Foreign Affairs by the Section de Statistique toward the end of January 1898. It was written by an Englishman who was most probably in contact with Foreign Ministry officials and who frequently supplied clandestine French agents with extremely accurate information on the attitudes of the British government.

The appearance of Frenchmen on the Upper Nile [the report began], if it should become a reality, will certainly

8. Sanderson, p. 265. Kitchener had already advanced as far as Berber with his Egyptian forces. He notified London toward the end of 1897 that he could not proceed further up the Nile without British reinforcements. Lord Cromer, the key British representative in Cairo, shared Kitchener's judgment.

9. *Ibid.*, p. 265.

10. Lillian M. Penson, " The Principles and Methods of Lord Salisbury's Foreign Policy," *Cambridge Historical Journal*, V (1935), 104. See also Penson, " The New Course in British Foreign Policy, 1892–1902," *Transactions of the Royal Historical Society*, XXV (1943), 121–38.

11. MAE, NS30: Campagne du Soudan, no. 6: Hanotaux to Courcel, 3 January 1898; no. 12: Hanotaux to Cogordan (Cairo), 4 January 1898.

12. *Ibid.*, no. 8: Geoffray to Hanotaux, 3 January 1898.

13. *Ibid.*, no. 53: Cogordan to Hanotaux, " Situation des troupes anglaises en Egypte et au Soudan," 1 February 1898.

14. Correspondance diplomatique de Félix Faure (CDFF), Hanotaux to Faure, an undated foreign policy brief presented to Faure by Hanotaux, most probably in February 1898.

be a very serious event. The British government has been occupied for some time with this possibility. When it finds itself in the presence of a fait accompli, it will ask if the French government has encouraged the agents in question and what the true goal of the expedition is.

It has been some time, as you well know, since the Under-secretary of State for Foreign Affairs declared in Commons that a French advance into the Upper Nile region would be considered an " unfriendly " act with regard to Great Britain. England is not disposed to depart from this attitude . . . .

I truly hope that an armed conflict can be avoided in these regions, but I cannot conceal that at the present moment the horizon appears somber from this vantage point.[15]

The horizon was just as somber on the French side of the Channel. Things looked even darker on 9 February when Baron Courcel reported that, in his judgment, the goal of the new British initiative was the " definitive affirmation of English power in Egypt and throughout the entire length of the Nile." [16] The Marchand mission had been planned initially to counter the Colville mission, a small British force which the French mistakenly believed was advancing to Fashoda in 1895. Now it was not a small band of British explorers en route to Fashoda but a massive Anglo-Egyptian army of close to 20,000. Because of this changed military situation and the sobering forecast of British intentions provided by French intelligence and Baron Courcel, Hanotaux was confronted with the necessity of reappraising French policy toward the Upper Nile.

The Times editorially suggested that the French Minister of Foreign Affairs, in view of the new situation in Egypt, might profitably " take an early opportunity of disavowing the erratic and inconvenient proceedings of his countrymen " in Africa.[17] It was not, of course, completely impossible for Hanotaux to do just

15. Ministère de la Guerre (MG), Service des renseignements, carton 13: Angleterre, 1898–1901, no. 527: " La France et l'Angleterre en Afrique," London, 14 January 1898. See also the excellent analyses contained in the following reports by the same agent: no. 642: " La Crise anglo-française," 22 February 1898; no. 643: " L'Angleterre, l'Abyssinie et les missions françaises," 20 February 1898; and no. 1314: " Politique africaine de l'Angleterre," 26 July 1898. Available information gives no indication of the definite identity of this agent.

16. *DDF*, XIV, no. 47: Courcel to Hanotaux, 9 February 1898.

17. Anon., " Our African Policy," *The Times* (London), 12 January 1898.

what *The Times* urged him to do; orders leaving Paris in January probably could have reached Marchand by September, and the Fashoda crisis could have been averted. Even though it was possible for Hanotaux to recall the Marchand mission, it would have been extremely difficult for a number of reasons. First of all, things had gone too far; too much effort and money had been invested in the project. Secondly, Hanotaux would have encountered the determined opposition of the Comité, the colonial group, and the Pavillon de Flore. Finally, a decision to recall Marchand would have been interpreted as a French defeat, and, in the wake of the Zola affair, Hanotaux was determined to demonstrate to the international community that France was not weakened by internal division.[18]

IV

Hanotaux made surprisingly few diplomatic preparations for the approaching confrontation with Great Britain. In 1897 and 1898 the *Bulletin du Comité de l'Afrique française* suggested that Hanotaux would never have " sent Marchand to Fashoda " without having secured the support of France's only ally, Imperial Russia.[19] This statement was a perfect reflection of what the Comité would have liked the Foreign Minister to do, but at the same time it completely distorted the actual situation. The Franco-Russian Alliance did not extend to the colonial sphere. France was not prepared to support Russian expansion in the Far East; Russia was not prepared to support French expansion in Africa. Thus, Hanotaux never requested Russian support for the Upper Nile project and the Czarist government never volunteered it.[20]

There remained the possibility of co-operation with Germany. Despite Alsace-Lorraine, the outstanding point of difference between France and Germany, the two countries had on occasion co-operated diplomatically against Great Britain in the colonial sphere. In 1894, for example, joint Franco-German pressure led Britain to abandon the Anglo-Congolese Treaty of that year. After 1894 intermittent signals reached Paris which indicated that Germany favored " parallel " policies or " practical collaboration " with France on specific colonial questions.[21] Although such initia-

18. See above, pp. 69–70.
19. *BCAF*, VII (November 1897) ; and VIII (February 1898).
20. Sanderson, p. 314.
21. An informed account of Franco-German relations during this period was written by Maurice Herbette in 1902 on the basis of his own experience as

tives invariably found no response in Paris, German diplomatists began to flirt with the possibility of enlisting French support for a scheme involving the partition of Portugal's possessions in Africa. On 18 June the French ambassador in Berlin discussed the German plan with Prince von Bülow, the Minister of Foreign Affairs, and then recommended that it be given serious consideration in Paris.[22] On the following day Count Münster submitted a *note verbale* to Hanotaux outlining the German project in some detail.[23]

On 15 June, just four days before Hanotaux learned of the German proposal, the Méline cabinet was overthrown. Although Hanotaux expressed an interest in the German overture, he made no final decision before departing from office because of his status as *ministre démissionnaire*. Before leaving the Quai d'Orsay, he collected together all of the diplomatic correspondence on the subject and had copies made for his own personal files.[24] Following the Fashoda crisis, Hanotaux used these documents in the construction of his apologia, *Fachoda*. In this book he excoriates his successor, Théophile Delcassé, for not pursuing the Portuguese colonies discussions and transforming them into a Franco-German rapprochement. He suggests that if this had been done, Germany would have sided with France during the Fashoda crisis.[25] This thesis, like much in Hanotaux's *Fachoda*, is tendentious and designed to exonerate himself of the responsibility for the Fashoda debacle. It is undoubtedly true that Delcassé terminated the Franco-German discussions, but there is absolutely no evidence to suggest that if they had been continued they could have formed the basis for a common front against Great Britain during the crisis. In addition, it seems clear that Hanotaux himself would never have tried to do what he suggested his successor do. Just before retiring from office, he told President Faure that French public opinion would utterly forbid co-operation with Germany against Great Britain.[26] Théophile Delcassé, after reviewing the documents on the subject, made precisely the same conclusion.[27]

ambassador in Berlin and the diplomatic correspondence at the Quai d'Orsay: MAE, Allemagne, NS26: Notes de Maurice Herbette.

22. *DDF*, XIV, no. 232: Noailles to Nisard, 19 June 1898.

23. *Ibid.*, no. 238: 19 June 1898.

24. MAE, Papiers Hanotaux, II: Notes et souvenirs, "Diverses affaires dans mes derniers jours au ministère."

25. Hanotaux, *Fachoda*, p. 132.

26. Félix Faure, "Fachoda (1898)," *Revue d'histoire diplomatique*, LXIX (1955), 31.

27. MAE, Papiers Delcassé, X: Allemagne, 1898–1911, nos. 1–16.

After the crisis Hanotaux often spoke of what he would have done if he had remained in office. In actual fact his diplomatic preparation was limited to one action: on 21 June 1898 he notified Cogordan, the French representative in Cairo, that Marchand and other French missions would soon arrive at Fashoda, and that he should therefore prepare for negotiations on the entire Egyptian question.[28] The meagerness of Hanotaux's diplomatic preparation suggests that even in 1898 he was less than wholeheartedly behind an initiative which he had strongly opposed in his first years as Minister of Foreign Affairs.[29] Hanotaux left to Delcassé the task of dealing with the consequences of a policy which the former had neither strongly supported nor effectively opposed during his years in office.

V

Delcassé had held no ministerial post since 1895, the year he had ceased to be Minister of Colonies. Since that time he had for the most part concerned himself with the colonial movement and his new interest, the navy. Hence, in 1898 most observers expected him to either become Minister of Marine or to return to the Ministry of Colonies.[30] When he was chosen as head of the Ministry of Foreign Affairs, there was some surprise in diplomatic circles.[31] The colonial milieu was exultant.[32]

The officers of the Marchand mission, having taken possession of Fashoda in the name of France on 12 July, were also pleased when they learned the name of the new Minister of Foreign Affairs in August. "We all knew M. Delcassé," Captain Baratier later wrote, "[he] was one of those rare men who, like M. Etienne, was au courant on colonial questions. Even more unusual, he was one of those who, at the moment of our departure [for Africa], was most disposed to accept the policy embodied in the mission." Marchand and his officers now believed that their mission had succeeded. "We are at Fashoda," exclaimed Baratier, " and England is still far from Omdurman! . . . The British dream is dead; the dream of Marchand is realized!"[33]

28. *DDF*, XIV, no. 236: Hanotaux to Cogordan, 21 June 1898.
29. See Sanderson, pp. 308–13.
30. NPFF, L: "Les Elections de 1898," 10 May 1898.
31. CDFF, no. 16: Montebello (St. Petersburg) to Faure, 20 August 1898.
32. *BCAF*, VIII (July and September 1898). Also, *La Quinzaine Coloniale*, 10 July 1898.
33. Aristide-E.-A. Baratier, *Souvenirs de la mission Marchand, III: Fachoda* (Paris, 1941), pp. 170–71.

The moment of triumph was marred, however, when at the climax of raising the Tricolor above the fort at Fashoda, the halyard snapped, and the symbol of the long-sought *présence française* in the Egyptian Sudan fell ingloriously to the ground. For many this event was a portent of future disaster.[34]

In Europe, also, there were ominous warnings. In a series of secret reports, the French military attaché in London, Colonel du Pontavice, suggested that Britain might well be preparing to take advantage of the internal dissensions created by the Dreyfus affair in France. To offset the harmful effects of the affair, du Pontavice went on to argue, France should clandestinely support projects to disrupt Great Britain internally.[35] A more sober analysis was offered by Geoffray, who, in the absence of Courcel, took responsibility for dealing with all questions of British policy. He warned on 20 August that there was a chauvinistic tide rising in Britain in the wake of Kitchener's victorious advance up the Nile.[36] This trend, Geoffray reported five days later, was beginning to be registered at the level of practical politics: a by-election in the Conservative stronghold of Southport had just returned a member of the opposition. Geoffray concluded with the following analysis:

> This election produced a distinct impression here precisely because local questions played only a secondary role and the campaign was devoted almost entirely to foreign policy questions. Isn't the defeat suffered by the Conservative candidate going to be interpreted as a public censure of the government's foreign policy? Will this not exercise a distinct influence on the attitude the cabinet takes regarding pending foreign policy questions? [37]

The most urgent foreign policy question pending for both the British and French cabinets was that of Egypt and the Upper Nile. In France another question was occupying the new Minister of Foreign Affairs, however. Soon after taking office Delcassé was caught up in the fanfare and glory of mediating between the two belligerents in the Spanish-American War. Consequently, he had

---

34. J. Emily, *Mission Marchand, journal de route* (Paris, 1913), pp. 133–34.
35. MAE, Grande Bretagne, NS8, du Pontavice to Courcel (forwarded to Paris), nos. 262, 276, 278, 279; 21 July, 3 August, 5 August, 10 August 1898.
36. *Ibid.*, no. 301: Geoffray to Delcassé, 20 August 1898.
37. MAE, Grande Bretagne, NS1: Politique intérieure, dossier générale, 1897–1902, no. 25: Geoffray to Delcassé, 25 August 1898.

devoted little time to the question of the approaching confrontation with Great Britain. After receiving the Great Cross of Charles III from a thankful Spanish monarch on 16 August, Delcassé, like most members of the Brisson cabinet, joined the general exodus from Paris which occurs each year during August, and journeyed to meet his wife on the Côte d'Azur.[38] The reports of du Pontavice and Geoffray, together with a request for a clarification of the Foreign Ministry's views on the Marchand mission from the new Minister of Colonies, Trouillot, lay unattended on the Foreign Minister's desk.[39] The corridors of the Quai d'Orsay, like the streets of Paris, were almost silent.

All was silent, but it was the quiet before the storm. In August 1898 the Third Republic was on the eve of two vast multidimensional crises, one domestic, the other international.

---

38. MAE, Lettres de Delcassé, Delcassé to Mme. Delcassé, 16 August 1898.
39. See below, pp. 96–97.

Chapter VI

DELCASSÉ, THE DREYFUS CRISIS, AND FASHODA, 30 AUGUST–19 SEPTEMBER 1898

The domestic crisis broke first. On 30 August the silence of the summer was shattered by an agence Havas release announcing that Colonel Henry, head of the Section de Statistique, had been arrested and charged with forging documents designed to incriminate Captain Dreyfus. All of the doubts sown by Zola in January now surfaced. In marked contrast to the summer months of 1898 when pro-Dreyfus agitation had almost subsided, public interest soared to a dramatic new high: in August less than 2,000 attended pro-Dreyfusard meetings in Paris, and a revisionist speaker was lucky to draw an audience of 200; in September over 25,000 Parisians rushed to pro-Dreyfusard demonstrations, and meetings attended by 2,000 to 5,000 cheering revisionists were not uncommon.[1] Respected newspapers like *Le Temps* and *Le Matin* reversed their previous positions and joined more extreme journals like *L'Aurore* and *La Petite République* in demanding revision. Toward the end of September a full-fledged anti-Dreyfusard movement emerged, but during the first two weeks of the month most observers were convinced that events had taken an irreversible and irresistible turn in the direction of revision.

On the international plane also, the *faux Henry* was a turning point. International interest in the affair had paralleled domestic interest, and during the summer of 1898 had declined substantially.[2] In September, however, the Quai d'Orsay was again flooded with reports similar to those received following "J'accuse" in January. At that time an overwhelming majority of European opinion had concluded that revision was morally necessary; now in September a consensus thought revision inevitable.[3] There was,

1. APP, Ba/106–7: Rapports quotidiens, August–September 1898.
2. See MAE, NS56: Affaire Dreyfus, IV, April–July 1898.
3. MAE, NS57: Affaire Dreyfus, V, August–September 1898. See especially

in addition, a new note of urgency abroad: the daily *Résumé de la presse étrangère*, prepared for the Minister of Foreign Affairs by his *cabinet*, quickly concluded that in the eyes of foreign observers the Third Republic was struggling through the most severe crisis of its troubled history.[4]

II

Théophile Delcassé was at the center of this crisis. Just hours before the public announcement of Henry's arrest, Delcassé learned the news and immediately grasped the significance of the situation. His first concern was preventing the Brisson cabinet from falling to pieces. Prime Minister Brisson, who had declared himself against revision at the time his cabinet was formed, now softened his stand. Minister of War Godefroy Cavaignac, however, immediately declared that he was prepared to resign rather than accept any alteration of the original verdict. Delcassé tried to act as a mediator between his two colleagues, and discussed the question with both of them in an effort to effect a compromise.[5] This effort collapsed, and on 3 September Cavaignac resigned.

Delcassé sounded out a number of the leaders of the French army and learned that Cavaignac's negative views were not universally accepted. Many generals, Delcassé wrote, believed that the worst thing the army could do would be to create the impression that the military establishment was trying to conceal something. He concluded that the upper echelons of the army would earnestly thank those who were energetic enough to take any measures " by which this plague tormenting us can be extirpated." [6] This is the view Delcassé presented at the cabinet meeting which took place on 5 September to consider the problems raised by Cavaignac's resignation and the question of Mme. Dreyfus' formal request of 3 September that her husband's case be reconsidered in

no. 63: Berlin to Paris, 31 August 1898; no. 74: Vienna to Paris, 2 September 1898; no. 82: Rome to Paris, 4 September 1898; no. 98: Geneva to Paris, 7 September 1898.

4. MAE, Papiers Delcassé, carton 16: Dossier de presse, September 1898.

5. MAE, Lettres de Delcassé, 31 August 1898. In the letters which he wrote to his wife between 31 August and the day she returned to Paris, 25 October, Delcassé expressed himself quite candidly and in great detail on the events of that period. Since all of these letters are addressed to Mme. Delcassé, they will be cited simply by their date.

6. *Ibid.*, 4 September 1898.

the light of the new situation created by the Henry forgery. Delcassé immediately sided with Brisson, the Prime Minister, and argued that some official support from the army should be obtained before deciding for revision. This, Brisson and Delcassé believed, would effectively counter any charge that revision was directed against the army itself.[7] The ministers then decided that General Zurlinden, a man whose sympathy for revision was known in official circles, would be offered the vacant post of Minister of War.

Zurlinden's acceptance filled Delcassé with hope. He was confident that the new Minister of War realized that there was " for the country as well as the army only one means of ending this terrible nightmare: it is to march resolutely toward truth . . . ." Delcassé was now convinced that " complete revision " was " inevitable," that Zurlinden would be willing to vote for revision, and that this would produce the unity he was seeking for the Brisson cabinet. On the basis of this unity, Delcassé believed, the Dreyfus affair could be relegated to the " juridical level " and the mounting public agitation would be terminated.[8]

Delcassé's behavior during the first week of September was quite unexpected. In 1894 he was one of the most violent anti-Dreyfus members of the Dupuy cabinet, the government which charged the army to indict the Jewish captain.[9] As Minister of Colonies it was Delcassé's duty to select from among French overseas possessions a place of exile suitable for the " traitor." His choice was symbolic: Devil's Island.[10] When he returned to office in 1898 his views had not changed: commitment to leaving the case unaltered was a prime prerequisite for inclusion in the Brisson cabinet. In addition, prior to September 1898 Delcassé was on good terms with rabid anti-Semitic elements of the emergent anti-Dreyfusard movement, and was, in the minds of revisionist leaders, one of the most determined opponents of revision.[11] In spite of

7. *Ibid.*, 5 September 1898. See also Henri Brisson, *Souvenirs: affaire Dreyfus* (Paris, 1908), pp. 28–37.

8. MAE, Lettres de Delcassé, 6 September 1898. See also Paléologue, *Journal de l'affaire Dreyfus*, pp. 132–41.

9. See above, pp. 31–32.

10. MAE, Lettres de Delcassé, 1 November 1894. Mme. Noguès adds in a footnote to this letter that once her father began to doubt the guilt of Dreyfus, " the thought that he had involuntarily contributed to the harshness of his [Dreyfus'] detention, weighed heavily on Delcassé." On Delcassé's key role, see Chapman, *Dreyfus Case*, p. iii.

11. Joseph Reinach, *Histoire de l'affaire Dreyfus*, IV (Paris, 1904), pp. 15–16.

this past record, Delcassé took a lead in the drive within the Brisson cabinet to open the way for revision, and his resolve never faltered in the difficult period of disagreement which followed the apparent consensus of the first week of September.

Delcassé's sustained and vigorous support for revision was the result of a number of factors. Like a majority of the Brisson government, he believed that the Henry forgery raised unsettling questions that needed juridical resolution, and that the mounting current of popular revisionist sentiment was irresistible.[12] Moreover, Delcassé's position as Minister of Foreign Affairs gave him access to reams of evidence indicating that the affair was progressively isolating France from the European community of nations.[13] His primary motive, however, was the desire to forestall a ministerial crisis which, as he often reiterated, might disrupt the continuity of French diplomacy at the exact moment when the Quai d'Orsay was faced with an accumulation of international difficulties.[14]

The first of these difficulties was the strain on Franco-Russian relations produced when Russian Foreign Minister Muraviev announced in a circular to all of the Great Powers the Czar's intention to call an international disarmament conference. This move was an affront to France because it was issued unilaterally by France's only ally, and because, as Delcassé put it, it condemned in advance any solution to the Alsace-Lorraine question by asking France to renounce the required instrument for the final resolution of this problem.[15] By the end of the first week in September, however, Delcassé had smoothed things over with the Russians to his satisfaction.[16] The rift with Russia was minor, however, when compared with the emergent crisis in Franco-British relations.

III

Fear of a ministerial crisis haunted the Minister of Foreign Affairs as he reviewed French policy toward the Upper Nile.

---

12. MAE, Lettres de Delcassé, 5 and 18 September 1898.

13. MAE, NS53–55: Affaire Dreyfus.

14. MAE, Lettres de Delcassé, 31 August 1898 (morning) ; 31 August 1898 (11:30 P.M.) ; 6 September 1898; 12 September 1898; 24 September 1898. See also Papiers Delcassé, III, Lettres de diplomates, Paul Cambon to Delcassé, 29 September 1898.

15. MAE, Papiers Delcassé, II: Russie, Delcassé's notes for a conversation with the Russian Prince Ouroussoff, 31 August 1898.

16. MAE, Lettres de Delcassé, 6 September 1898.

Soon after Delcassé took office, the new Minister of Colonies, Georges Trouillot, wrote to him requesting a clarification of the Quai d'Orsay's position on the Marchand mission.[17] Two weeks later Trouillot underlined the urgency of the situation by informing Delcassé that Marchand was near Fashoda and "found the route clear before him."[18] In 20 July, Nisard, head of the Direction Politique at the Ministry of Foreign Affairs, stated that his department needed cartographic information so that Marchand's advance could be precisely plotted,[19] and soon after that Delcassé approved a 25,000-franc expenditure from the *fonds secrets* for the "transportation of arms and ammunition destined for the Marchand mission."[20] Although these actions showed that Delcassé was aware of the Upper Nile problem, they scarcely clarified the policy of the Ministry of Foreign Affairs.

During the first week of September when most of Delcassé's time was taken up by the affair, alarming reports reached Paris which turned his attention more and more toward the Upper Nile. First of all, the Quai d'Orsay learned that the Mahdists had been demolished by the advancing Anglo-Egyptian army at the battle of Khartoum on 2 September. Secondly, from both London and Berlin came reports that a thaw was occurring in Anglo-German relations. Geoffray reported that there was a general feeling in London that the rapprochement with Germany was an arrangement designed to "consolidate and consecrate the establishment of the English in Egypt."[21] From Berlin came news that William II had just reminded an assembly of German troops of the "confraternity of arms between the English and the Germans" which dated back to Waterloo, and had then led the troops in a cheer saluting British victories in the Sudan.[22]

Delcassé's first action was to dispatch telegrams to both London and Berlin which ordered French diplomats in those capitals to report immediately any developments in the "rapprochement which appears to be occurring at this moment between Germany

17. MC, Afrique III, 32b, no. 72: Delcassé to Trouillot, 7 September 1898. A marginal note indicates that this was Delcassé's first reply to a written request made by Trouillot in June.

18. *Ibid.*, no. 66: Trouillot to Delcassé, 13 July 1898.

19. *Ibid.*, no. 67: Nisard to Trouillot, 20 July 1898.

20. *Ibid.*, no. 68: Delcassé to Trouillot, 27 July 1898.

21. MAE, Allemagne, NS60: Relations avec l'Angleterre, 1897–1914, no. 30: Geoffray to Delcassé, 30 September 1898.

22. *Ibid.*, no. 33: Berlin to Delcassé, received 5 September 1898.

and England." [23] The Foreign Minister then drafted a long memorandum explicitly outlining for the first time his views on the Marchand mission.

As of 7 September Delcassé viewed the situation in the following manner. Things had changed, he believed, since the early years of the Upper Nile project. In Africa, the Anglo-Egyptian victory at Khartoum removed the last military advantage enjoyed by Marchand and shifted the local balance of power in favor of Kitchener. In Europe, he added, France was at a disadvantage because of the apparent détente in Anglo-German relations.[24] Delcassé feared that in exchange for concessions in other parts of Africa, Britain had received a " carte blanche in Egypt " from Germany.[25] He was also alarmed by the domestic political situation in Britain and its possible impact on British foreign policy. " Is it necessary to conclude," Delcassé wrote, " that England is going to take advantage of the seizure of Khartoum to proclaim a protectorate in the Nile Valley? Indeed, I think that such a *coup d'éclat* would gratify the English chauvinists, and perhaps consolidate the Salisbury ministry." [26]

On the basis of the changed situation, Delcassé concluded that the moment was unfavorable for a reopening of the Egyptian question, and that the Marchand mission should be ordered to stop its advance at some point short of Fashoda.[27] Such a move, Delcassé undoubtedly hoped, would avert a confrontation with Great Britain in which France would be at a distinct disadvantage.

This view, which was communicated to the Ministry of Colonies on 7 September, amounted to a renunciation of the very policy that Delcassé himself had so vigorously supported in his early years at the Pavillon de Flore.[28] The new Minister of Foreign Affairs was now much more concerned with the continental implications of French policy, and was probably already dreaming of the day when Great Britain could be brought into the Franco-Russian alliance.[29] With Delcassé in this frame of mind, it is not

23. *Ibid.*, no. 35: Delcassé to London (with a copy to Berlin), 6 September 1898.
24. MC, Afrique III, 32a, no. 72: Delcassé to Trouillot, 7 September 1898.
25. MAE, Lettres de Delcassé, 7 September 1898.
26. *Ibid.*
27. MC, Afrique III, 32a, no. 72: Delcassé to Trouillot, 7 September 1898.
28. See above, pp. 24–32.
29. See below, pp. 120–26 for a detailed discussion of this point.

surprising that Ambassador Monson, after his first discussion with the French Foreign Minister on 7 September on the question of the Upper Nile, concluded that France would admit British claims to the Egyptian Sudan without provoking a serious incident. Monson cautiously added, however, that Delcassé would remain conciliatory only so long as his hand was not forced by domestic pressures.[30]

IV

Domestic pressure was already mounting. During the first three weeks of September the Dreyfus affair still captured the headlines, but interest in the changing situation in the Sudan had begun to rise. The first press commentaries came in the wake of Kitchener's victory over the Mahdists on 2 September. Coverage increased as the rumor spread that the victorious Anglo-Egyptian army would soon encounter a French force under Marchand at some point on the Upper Nile. Leaders of the colonial movement immediately alerted the French public to the significance of these events. Eugène Etienne expressed the views of the Chamber's colonial group in a long article published in La Dépêche Coloniale. The real issue, Etienne wrote, was not the military victory at Khartoum but rather the entire future of Egypt, and the moment was now at hand for the initiation of serious diplomatic negotiations between France and Great Britain on that subject. The right wing press, Le Soleil, Le Gaulois, L'Eclair, and La Patrie, as well as influential moderate journals like Le Figaro, Le Temps, and Le Matin, took substantially the same position: the time had come, according to writers in these papers, for the resolution of a situation which had complicated Franco-British relations since the British occupation of Cairo in 1882.[31]

The Comité de l'Afrique française also swung into action. Colonel Monteil, who had retired from the army to devote his full time to the colonial movement, proclaimed before a crowd of enthusiasts that the program of the Marchand mission was " identical " with the project which had originally been entrusted to him in 1893. Marchand, concluded Monteil, was not merely engaged in the " realization of an explorer's dream," but was

30. PRO, FO 78/5050, no. 441: Monson to Salisbury, 8 September 1898.
31. Rachael Arié, " L'Opinion publique en France et l'affaire de Fachoda," Revue d'histoire des colonies, XLI (1954), 345–47.

executing a "deliberate and premeditated official governmental act with a precisely determined goal." [32] And Robert de Caix, the leading writer and an official spokesman for the Comité, warned that a crisis of exceptional gravity was in the offing and counseled the government to gird itself for the shock. [33]

Was the Brisson cabinet prepared to meet the shock of a confrontation with Britain in the wake of the blows it was already enduring because of the Dreyfus affair? This was the problem which increasingly disturbed the colonialist milieu in September 1898. "The primary question at the present time," wrote Lucien Dyé, who corresponded regularly with Terrier, and was one of the Comité's best-informed members, "is if our government will sustain the struggle on the diplomatic plane with the same energy as our officers on the African continent." Dyé then went on to speculate on whether or not "internal difficulties could possibly prevent our external policy from following its regular course and resolving the grave questions posed at the present time." [34]

Internal questions were already interfering with the regular course of French foreign policy. The blow of the *faux Henry* had fallen heavily on the French intelligence service, an organization which regularly provided the Quai d'Orsay with military and political intelligence which had proved both reliable and useful in the past. [35] Maurice Paléologue, the Ministry of Foreign Affairs'

32. MAE, Papiers Delcassé, carton 16: Résumé de la presse française, 19 September 1898.
33. Robert de Caix, "Après le prise de Khartoum," *BCAF*, VIII (September 1898), 278–81.
34. BI, Fonds Terrier, 5897, Dyé to Terrier, 19 September 1898.
35. See above, pp. 73–74, for one example of the accuracy of the intelligence service's information. The impact of clandestinely acquired information on the formulation of French foreign policy remains something of a mystery, a mystery which has never attracted as much attention as the detective aspect of the Dreyfus affair but is nevertheless one which deserves systematic study. My investigation has revealed that the Section de Statistique frequently acquired accurate information which was regularly passed on to the Ministry of Foreign Affairs. It seems logical to conclude that consistently accurate information on the intentions of foreign powers would prove useful to policy-makers, but I have been unable to find in either the Hanotaux or Delcassé papers any explicit reflections on the role which such information might have played in their decisions. The problem is complicated by the fact that the records housed at the Quai d'Orsay concerning the Foreign Ministry's relations with the military intelligence group were destroyed in 1940. All that remains, therefore, are the dossiers of intelligence reports stored at the Service historique de l'armée (Château Vincennes), and there are some serious gaps in these for the period before 1898. When the archives are opened for the period

special assistant for intelligence, arrived at the rue St. Dominique headquarters of the Section de Statistique on 5 September only to find its offices and personnel in a state of disarray.[36] The small agency's normal routine of collecting and transmitting intelligence to the Ministries of War and Foreign Affairs seemed to have been seriously disrupted, and throughout September the flow of vital information on the intentions of foreign powers which normally emanated from these offices was reduced to a trickle.[37]

At the Quai d'Orsay the Dreyfus affair was also taking its toll. On 12 September Delcassé complained that the domestic situation was needlessly complicating his work at the Ministry of Foreign Affairs. "What decisions can be taken," Delcassé despairingly wrote, "when at any moment the cabinet could resign?" "What a fate burdens this country," he continued; "it leaves one scandal behind only to fall into another which halts all political life."[38] Unless the affair were relegated to the juridical plane, Delcassé argued at a cabinet meeting on 13 September, "I see only disorder, confusion, discredit—all to the profit of foreign powers."[39] And on the following day, the Foreign Minister, after writing that not since 1870 had "there been a parallel accumulation of such grave questions to resolve," lashed out against the internal situation: "I had no need for the distraction of the Dreyfus Affair. It's so sad!"[40]

Delcassé had not shaken this mood when on 18 September he again discussed the Fashoda question with the British ambassador. On 9 September Monson was instructed by Salisbury to "point out

after 1900, however, it will be possible to make a systematic investigation of the intelligence archives over a decade or more and compare these reports with the diplomatic correspondence in an effort to discover the role of clandestine intelligence in the formulation of policy.

36. Paléologue, *Journal de l'affaire Dreyfus*, pp. 135–36.

37. MG, Service des renseignements, carton 13: Angleterre, 1898–1901. There are fewer reports for September, a month when tension was on the increase, than for August, a month of relatively little international tension. Not until October did the Section de Statistique recover from the setback of losing its chief, Colonel Henry, and begin to report regularly on British intentions regarding the Egyptian Sudan and the crisis with France.

38. MAE, Lettres de Delcassé, 12 September 1898.

39. *Ibid.*, 13 September 1898.

40. *Ibid.*, 14 September 1898. See also Paléologue, *Journal de l'affaire Dreyfus*, pp. 140–41; and *Félix Faure à l'Elysée* (*Souvenirs de Louis Le Gall*), ed. Charles Braibant (Paris, 1963), pp. 202–12. Hereafter cited as *Souvenirs de Louis Le Gall*. Paléologue and Le Gall both indicate that the domestic situation weighed heavily on foreign policy decision-makers during both September and October.

that all the territories which were subject to the Khalifa pass by
the events of last week to the British and Egyptian governments
by right of conquest. We do not consider this right open to
discussion." [41] On the following day these views were transmitted
to Delcassé. The French Foreign Minister, who now seems to
have lost his earlier hope that Marchand might halt before reaching Fashoda, quickly retorted: " If Marchand is at Fashoda, his
' rights ' are exactly the same as those of Kitchener at Khartoum." [42]

On 18 September when Delcassé renewed this line of argument,
Monson simply referred him to a most explicit statement of British
policy toward the Upper Nile: the Grey Declaration of 1895.[43]
Delcassé replied by suggesting that there was really no such thing
as the Marchand mission because Marchand was subordinate to
Liotard, and the Liotard mission, Delcassé continued, was launched
in 1893, long before the Grey Declaration had made known
Britain's uncompromising position on the Upper Nile.

This curious blend of sophistic logic and tendentious history
was offered up by a man who well knew the real facts. The Monteil mission, not the Liotard mission, had been launched in 1893
by Delcassé himself when he was Undersecretary of State for
Colonies; Monteil's goal was clearly an open confrontation with
Great Britain and a reopening of the Egyptian question. A mission
headed by Liotard had been accepted toward the end of 1894 by
the Dupuy ministry largely because of pressure from Delcassé.
But this mission was distinct from the Marchand project, which
was accepted by the Quai d'Orsay toward the end of 1895, months
after the Grey Declaration had made the gravity of the decision
clear.[44] Marchand had been technically subordinate to Liotard
in the early phases of his mission, but this special relationship had
ended in November 1897.[45] Although Delcassé was not in office
at the time the Marchand mission was launched, he was probably
au courant as to its history and goals. The prosaic facts, however,
were lost in a cloud of rhetoric as Delcassé sought to score diplomatic debating points against the British ambassador.

The rhetoric of the diplomatic debate should not obscure Del-

41. PRO, FO 141/336, Salisbury to Monson, 9 September 1898. "Khalifa"
was the title used by the British for the leader of the Mahdist State.
42. *Ibid.*, no. 131: Monson to Salisbury, 10 September 1898.
43. See above, pp. 34–35.
44. See above, pp. 29–32 and pp. 39–44.
45. See above, pp. 49–51; and Marchand, *Le Matin*, 20 June 1905.

cassé's real concerns. One of these was the safety of Marchand and his men. The Foreign Minister feared that the British would treat Marchand as a " pirate," and that " a bloody conflict whose consequences would be difficult to limit " might ensue.[46] In addition, Delcassé continued to be concerned about the deteriorating domestic situation in France.

V

During the first week of September Delcassé had been hopeful that a resolute cabinet decision for revision would quickly remove the affair from the field of public controversy, and that such a move would decrease the threat of a ministerial crisis. On 17 September the Brisson ministry moved in this direction by voting to submit the Dreyfus case to a three-man juridical board for reconsideration. This decision, however, failed to remove the affair from the arena of public debate or to secure the position of the cabinet.

General Zurlinden, in a complete about-face, resigned rather than submit to the 17 September decision. Hence, the first step toward revision was taken without the symbolic approval of the army in the person of a military Minister of War. These circumstances convinced a large segment of the French population that the government of the Republic was in the hands of a sinister conspiracy whose ultimate aim was to dismantle the military establishment of the nation and leave France vulnerable to foreign attack.[47] This group formed the basis of support for the emergent nationalist movement.

As it became clear that Zurlinden would not vote for revision, the nationalist movement gained new momentum.[48] In the week immediately following the news of the Henry forgery, Charles Maurras threw the weight of his polemical and literary talents against the general tide of revisionist sentiment and, in a widely publicized Le Gaulois article, glorified Colonel Henry's deed as a

---

46. MAE, Lettres de Delcassé, 19 September 1898.

47. This thesis is most clearly stated in the voluminous study of Godefroy Cavaignac's daughter, Mme. Henriette Dardenne, L'Affaire Dreyfus, crise de conscience national, BN, n. a. fr. 13499, pp. 3–55.

48. AN, F⁷ 12870: Ligue des patriotes, pp. 1–20, gives a summary of this phase of the Ligue's development. F⁷ 12449: Ligue des patriotes, 1889–1898 gives detailed information on the various abortive attempts to reconstitute the Ligue between 1889 and 1898.

supremely patriotic act.[49] The mystique of the " *faux patriotique* " breathed new life into the emergent nationalist right, and during the second week of September nationalist gangs disrupted a number of staged Dreyfusard demonstrations.[50] Eight days after the 17 September decision, between 3,000 and 4,000 excited demonstrators united at the Salle Guyenet to formally reconstitute the Ligue des patriotes under the leadership of Paul Déroulède.[51] Déroulède's old supporters, who had remained in contact since the Ligue des patriotes was first legally prescribed in 1889, were now joined by followers of Guerin's Ligue antisémitique and by the backers of Henri de Rochefort.[52] A new political force, which Delcassé labeled the " debris of Boulangism," had entered the scene.[53] Its long-range goal was the reconstruction of France and the reassertion of French power in the world; its more immediate objective was the overthrow of the Brisson cabinet.[54]

The Brisson cabinet was also coming under increasing fire from the Dreyfusard left. Two of the principal leaders of this group, Georges Clemenceau and Jean Jaurès, the editors of *L'Aurore* and *La Petite République*, attacked Brisson for not acting more quickly and for not suppressing the rising violence perpetrated by the anti-Dreyfusard right.[55] Popular Dreyfusard demonstrators like Joindy, Pressensé, and Sebastian Faure severely criticized the Brisson cabinet for its " deplorable indecision." [56]

By 20 September French society was increasingly polarized over the Dreyfus affair, and the extremist elements on the right and the left were taking the lead in pushing the situation closer and closer toward massive open violence: clashes in the streets of Paris between Dreyfusard and anti-Dreyfusard demonstrators were occurring almost daily. Events seemed to be moving rapidly toward

49. The importance of Maurras' act has been underlined by Ernst Nolte, *Three Faces of Fascism* (New York, 1966), p. 56.

50. APP, Ba/107: Rapport quotidien, 7 September–21 September 1898. The clashes of 8, 15, and 17 September were especially violent.

51. The Salle Guyenet was appropriately located on the avenue de la Grande Armée.

52. *Ibid.*, 26 September 1898. See also F[7] 12882: Antisémitisme, 1897–1905; and *La Libre Parole*, 26 September 1898.

53. MAE, Lettres de Delcassé, 17 September 1898.

54. APP, Ba/107: Rapport quotidien, 26 September; and AN, F[7] 12870, Ligue des patriotes, 1 and 8 October 1898.

55. *L'Aurore*, 10, 12, and 17 September 1898; and *La Petite République*, 7 and 12 September 1898.

56. APP, Ba/107: Rapport quotidien, 12 September–20 September 1898.

a ministerial crisis: the left was alienated because Brisson had not acted quickly enough; the right was alienated because the cabinet had acted at all; and moderate members of the parliamentary elite were alarmed because the ministry appeared irresolute and weak in the face of growing domestic disorder.

In spite of the increasingly grave situation, Delcassé believed that it was still possible to prevent the fall of the cabinet. He envisioned two governmental courses of action: in France, vigorous suppression of the domestic strife; on the international scene, a carefully staged diplomatic victory.[57] Only an indefatigable optimist and a man of supreme confidence in his own diplomatic talent like Delcassé could hope to garner anything resembling a victory from the Fashoda situation. Nevertheless, he appears to have clung to this hope from the beginning of September until the last half of October.[58] This is not to say that the French Foreign Minister ever thought the program of the colonialist milieu had any chance of success. As early as 7 September Delcassé had abandoned all hope of reopening the Egyptian question or of making substantial territorial gains, and he never again flirted with this grandiose scheme. The question was never if Marchand should be recalled; had it been possible to communicate with Marchand during the first week of September, Delcassé would probably have ordered him not to advance to Fashoda.[59] The question was rather when and under what conditions Marchand would depart Fashoda.

The French Foreign Minister seems to have relied upon Lord Salisbury's reputation for making " graceful concessions," and hoped that some territorial gains in the Bahr-el-Ghazal would be granted France following a phase of extended negotiations. All of this, Delcassé seems to have believed, could have been presented to the French Chamber and the public as a diplomatic success.[60]

Delcassé's assessment of Lord Salisbury was not without foundation. Robert Marquis of Salisbury, who was 68 in 1898 and had been Prime Minister and Foreign Minister on two occasions in the past, was trained in the school of Old Diplomacy. The aging Tory was practiced in the art of extended and polite diplomatic

57. MAE, Lettres de Delcassé, 17 and 25 September 1898; 6 October 1898.
58. *Ibid*., 6 and 21 September 1898; and 4, 5, 7, and 20 October 1898.
59. See above, pp. 84–85.
60. MAE, Lettres de Delcassé, 4, 5, and 7 October 1898.

bouts of negotiations and counternegotiations, and believed that a representative of one of the Great Powers should never be pushed to the wall in a crisis. He abhored war as an event which signaled the failure of diplomacy.[61] When Salisbury first sent Monson instructions on 9 September, he left open the possibility of negotiating with France some territorial concession near the Upper Nile, and he tried to keep this option open until the climactic British cabinet meeting of 28 October.[62]

Thus, as long as events remained within the framework set by the Old Diplomacy, Delcassé's expectation of some face-saving compensation in return for the recall of Marchand was not completely out of the question. Toward the end of September, however, forces were at work which would soon drastically disrupt the venerable traditions of quiet cabinet diplomacy by injecting the volatile issues of the international confrontation into the domestic politics of both France and Great Britain.

61. Penson, "Lord Salisbury's Foreign Policy," pp. 87–106. See also Penson's *Foreign Affairs under the Third Marquess of Salisbury* (London, 1962); and A. L. Kennedy, *Salisbury, 1830–1903* (London, 1963).
62. Andrew, *Théophile Delcassé*, pp. 100–101.

CHAPTER VII

THE DOMESTIC AND INTERNATIONAL CRISES
CONVERGE, 20 SEPTEMBER–4 NOVEMBER 1898

Captain Jean-Baptiste Marchand was more concerned about the local situation in Africa than the changing domestic picture in Europe. Late on 18 September Marchand received a message addressed to the " Chief of the European Expedition at Fashoda " and signed by Kitchener. In the most blunt terms, the commander of the Anglo-Egyptian army announced that he had destroyed the Mahdist army, " re-occupied the country," and was now advancing in force to Fashoda.[1] Marchand, who was stung by Kitchener's arrogance, replied in kind. In a message which bore the seal of " Afrique centrale française," Marchand, who styled himself " Commissaire du governement français sur le Haut Nil et Bahr-el-Ghazal," informed Kitchener that the Bahr-el-Ghazal and the surrounding area had been occupied in the name of the French government, and that it had formally come under French protection on 3 September by a treaty with native tribes of the area. Thus, Marchand proudly concluded, he would be happy to welcome Kitchener to Fashoda " *au nom de la France.*" [2]

Marchand was no less arrogant when he encountered Kitchener personally on 19 September. Kitchener formally protested France's " infringement of the rights of Egypt and Great Britain." Marchand retorted that he had occupied the area at the orders of his government and that he intended to remain there unless his earlier orders were countermanded by Paris. Kitchener replied that he had been ordered " to re-establish Egyptian authority in the Fashoda Murdirieh," and after reminding Marchand that he was in possession of superior force, demanded whether the French captain " was prepared . . . to resist the execution of those orders."

1. *DDF*, XIV, Appendix I, no. 1: Kitchener to Marchand, 18 September 1898.
2. PRO, FO 78/5051, Marchand to Kitchener, 19 September 1898.

To this Marchand answered that he and his men would " die at their posts " if such a course became necessary.[3]

Marchand, however, was convinced that the British would not employ their superior military force. The proud captain fully expected the weight of French diplomacy to offset the balance of local military power, and continued to believe that events would follow the course which the planners of his mission had outlined in 1895. " If I am not mistaken," Marchand reported in a private letter to Delcassé, " Great Britain will offer absolutely no objection to the convening of the European conference [to deal with the Egyptian question], and will even allow France to hold provisionally the Bahr-el-Ghazal while waiting for the definitive and total [British] evacuation of Egypt. [Britain] will fix a time limit for the evacuation of perhaps 18 to 20 months . . . ." [4]

Marchand's mood darkened considerably, however, after reading recent Paris newspapers provided him by Kitchener. " One hour after we opened the French papers," he later recalled, " the ten French officers were trembling and weeping. We learned then and there that the terrible Dreyfus affair had been opened with its dreadful campaign of infamies, and for thirty-six hours not one of us was able to say anything to the others." [5]

II

Despite some apprehension about the deleterious effects of the domestic situation in Paris, Marchand's key supporters in the French colonial movement were initially as optimistic as the African adventurer himself. The mood at the rue de la Ville l'Evêque headquarters of the Comité de l'Afrique française is captured in a letter received by secretary-general Terrier from Lucien Dyé the very day Marchand first spoke with Kitchener.

I am persuaded that upon arriving at Fashoda the English have found our " Congo-Nile " column strongly established

3. PRO, FO 141/333, no. 153: Rodd to Salisbury, 29 September 1898 (enclosing Kitchener to Rodd, 21 September 1898). Cited by Sanderson, p. 334. See also Emily, " A Fachoda, le 19 Septembre 1898," BCAF, LXVI (March 1937), 124–27, 192–94; Emily, Mission Marchand, p. 182; and Marchand's own account of the encounter with Kitchener, Le Figaro, 26 August 1904.

4. MAE, Papiers Delcassé, XIII: Angleterre I: Fachoda 1898, no. 37: Marchand to Delcassé, 10 October 1898.

5. Marchand to Forain, 6 November 1898, published in Le Figaro, 20 November 1898. Cited by Andrew, Théophile Delcassé, p. 93.

at this point . . . . Independent of his original mission, with its perfectly-trained personnel, he [Marchand] must have been joined by three missions of reinforcements and supplies which were subsequently sent from France . . . . Methodically prepared, the occupation of the entire Bahr-el-Ghazal must be an established fact at the present moment.

On the other branch of the Nile I have every reason to believe that the Ethiopians have made contact with our officers . . . .

In these excellent conditions I am persuaded that Marchand will not cede an inch of conquered territory . . . .[6]

Also determined that Marchand should hold his ground was Gustave Binger, the Comité's key civilian contact within the official French foreign policy establishment.[7] Binger's power and influence at the Ministry of Colonies had reached a new high when in the summer of 1898 Monson labeled him the " acting chief of the Colonial Department "; his position remained intact following the constitution of the Brisson ministry.[8] Soon after Binger briefed Georges Trouillot on the situation in the Egyptian Sudan, the inexperienced new Minister of Colonies became a convinced supporter of the Upper Nile project.[9] In September and October 1898 Trouillot accepted Binger's lead and made an uncompromising line on Fashoda the official policy of the Ministry of Colonies.[10]

Following Delcassé's 7 September policy statement to the Ministry of Colonies, tension between the Pavillon de Flore and the Quai d'Orsay increased sharply. Trouillot made no effort to comply with Delcassé's wishes and order Marchand not to advance, and, despite repeated requests, Delcassé refused to communicate to the Ministry of Colonies any information on his nego-

6. BI, Fonds Terrier, 5897, Dyé to Terrier, 19 September 1897.

7. See above, pp. 50–51.

8. CCO, Salisbury Papers, A/116, no. 32: Monson to Salisbury, 27 May 1898; and no. 38: same to same, 5 July 1898. In the latter Monson spoke of the " great influence " exercised by the " permanent officials " in the newly constituted Brisson cabinet.

9. DDF, XIV, no. 246: Trouillot to Delcassé, 4 July 1898.

10. Ibid., no. 252: Trouillot to Delcassé, 15 September 1898; and MC, Afrique III, 33, no. 10: same to same, 22 October, and no. 11: 29 October 1898. Most of these communications were drafted by Binger's department, the Bureau de l'Afrique, and signed by Trouillot. The rough drafts remain in the colonial archives.

tiations with the British.[11] The situation was further complicated because Trouillot believed that Brisson and Delcassé were withholding from him vital information on the Dreyfus case.[12]

The simmering conflict between Trouillot and Delcassé seems to have come to a head on 26 September, the day the Fashoda situation was first discussed at a formal meeting of the Brisson cabinet. The day before, Monson had informed Delcassé of the Marchand-Kitchener encounter and had read aloud a telegram from Kitchener which sought to demonstrate that " Marchand's position at Fashoda is as impossible as it is absurd " because of the French expedition's lack of ammunition and supplies.[13] If Delcassé described Marchand's position to members of the cabinet in similar terms—and it is likely that he did—Trouillot very probably took grave exception. The Ministry of Colonies was already preparing a long report which sought to demonstrate that Marchand was well provisioned (which indeed he was), and that at least three relief missions would soon reach Fashoda.[14] Faced with a difference of opinion between its foreign policy experts, the Brisson cabinet decided to request a situation report from Marchand, and to defer any decision on Fashoda until after it reached Paris.[15]

Delcassé's conflict with the Ministry of Colonies had unfortunate consequences. Following the 26 September cabinet meeting, Trouillot, probably under the influence of his chief African adviser

11. MC, Afrique III, 32b, Nisard to Trouillot, 19 September 1898; and Delcassé to Trouillot, 15 October 1898. These two documents, which contain no information on the course of Franco-British negotiations, are the only responses which the Quai d'Orsay seems to have made to the urgent requests for information received from the Ministry of Colonies on 15 September, 8 October, and 22 October 1898.

12. Johnson, *France and the Dreyfus Affair*, p. 149. The information in question was very probably the much-discussed *dossier diplomatique* which Delcassé showed to Zürlinden on 17 September 1898 in an effort to convince the general that he should vote for revision. Although both Delcassé and Paléologue spoke often of the *dossier diplomatique* concerning the affair, French archivists, according to M. Georges Dethan, have never found such a collection of documents.

13. *British Documents on the Origins of the War, 1898–1914*, I (London, 1927), no. 193: Rodd to Salisbury, 25 September 1898 (enclosing Kitchener to Rodd telegram of 24 September 1898).

14. MAE, Papiers Delcassé, XIII, " Organization et renforcement de la mission Marchand," 10 October 1898. This document was not communicated in the normal manner from the Ministry of Colonies to the Ministry of Foreign Affairs. I have been unable to find a copy of it in the official archives of either ministry. It was probably given to Delcassé personally by Trouillot.

15. *DDF*, XIV, no. 384: note du ministre, 27 September 1898.

Binger, decided to step up pressure on the Ministry of Foreign Affairs by focusing public attention on Fashoda. A reporter from the right-wing journal *Le Gaulois* was summoned to the Pavillon de Flore and was briefed on previously undisclosed facts concerning the Marchand-Kitchener encounter. This move, which had not been cleared with the Ministry of Foreign Affairs, led to the publication of a sharply anti-British *Le Gaulois* article on 28 September. Trouillot's statement was immediately picked up and transformed into dramatic headline news by the British press. *The Times*, the *Morning Post*, and the *Evening News*, all Conservative journals, saw the Minister of Colonies' revelations as an official statement of French policy, and demanded an immediate public clarification of British policy.[16]

Trouillot's unauthorized disclosure drastically altered the framework of the Franco-British diplomatic dialogue. Since the opening of negotiations, both Lord Salisbury's government and the Ministry of Foreign Affairs had made a determined effort to keep the details of their discussions on the level of cabinet diplomacy. Both Delcassé and Salisbury distrusted the public, and believed that any open presentation of an official point of view would needlessly restrict their freedom. Nevertheless, both men were under increasing pressure to make their official positions public. Trouillot's leak to the press tipped the balance: Lord Salisbury informed Delcassé through Monson that " immediate communication of the facts to the public was inevitable." [17] Then, in an unprecedented move, the British government announced its intention to publish a diplomatic *Blue Book* on the Fashoda question before the dispute had run its course.[18] Delcassé intensely distrusted " negotiating in public," but he had no other choice.[19] Hence, the Quai d'Orsay began preparation of a *Livre jaune*, and planned its publication for 24 October, just before the French Chamber was scheduled to

16. MAE, Lettres de Delcassé, 29 September 1898; and PRO, FO 27/3397, no. 486: Monson to Salisbury, 28 September 1898. See also T. W. Riker, " A Survey of British Policy in the Fashoda Crisis," *Political Science Quarterly*, XLIV (1929), 54–78.

17. MAE, Lettres de Delcassé, 29 September 1898.

18. Sanderson, p. 347. *Egypt No. 2 (1898)* [*C.–9054*]: *Correspondence with the French Government Respecting the Valley of the Nile* was issued on 10 October, and *Egypt No. 3 (1898)* [*C.–9055*] was issued on 23 October. Normal diplomatic practice required that selected diplomatic documents be published only after a diplomatic dispute was resolved.

19. MAE, Lettres de Delcassé, 2 October 1898.

reconvene. No longer could the diplomatic negotiations be insulated from the increasing heat of public debate: in Britain, politicians like Asquith, Bryce, and Hicks Beech made belligerent speeches; in France, by 4 October two deputies had announced interpellations on the Fashoda question.[20]

Delcassé was infuriated by Trouillot's unilateral decision to flout publicly the will of the Ministry of Foreign Affairs. He was frankly frightened by the British response.[21] For the first time the prospect of war with Great Britain over the Upper Nile invaded the French Foreign Minister's consciousness, and the idea of a British "ultimatum" calling for an immediate withdrawal of Marchand increasingly haunted him.[22] During the opening minutes of his 30 September meeting with Monson, Delcassé sensed that the British ambassador was carrying a written ultimatum in his coat.[23] In an effort to prevent the document from being delivered, Delcassé quickly declared that France would go to war rather than swallow "such an insult to the national honour."[24] "I am able to sacrifice material interests," the agitated Foreign Minister continued, "but in my hands the national honor will remain intact. It is not from the minister before you that you can expect a capitulation."[25]

Monson immediately grasped the reality behind Delcassé's bombastic show of patriotism. He reported to Salisbury that the French Foreign Minister was definitely not "bluffing" and that "he thoroughly meant what he said." Delcassé's motives, Monson continued, were closely linked to the critical domestic situation in France:

> Delcassé has judged quite correctly as to the utter impossibility of the French Government conceding the recall of M. Marchand. Such a step would involve, I am convinced, the immediate fall of the Cabinet, and would be disavowed by

20. *Ibid.*, 4 October 1898; *Annual Register* (London), 1898, pp. 162–68, gives a brief summary of the speeches of British politicians on Fashoda.

21. MAE, Lettres de Delcassé, 31 September 1898; and CCO, Salisbury Papers, A/116, no. 52: Monson to Salisbury, 14 October 1898.

22. Delcassé's fear of a British ultimatum may have stemmed from mistaken information in an Italian diplomatic message intercepted by the French and presented to the Foreign Minister on 30 September; see Andrew, *Théophile Delcassé*, pp. 98–99.

23. MAE, Lettres de Delcassé, 1 October 1898.

24. PRO, FO 78/5051, no. 160: Monson to Salisbury, 30 September 1898.

25. MAE, Lettres de Delcassé, 1 October 1898.

their successors. The irritation of the Army and of a large portion of the public over the Dreyfus " affair," renders the situation of the Government more than usually delicate; and any symptom of weakness on the Fashoda question would be the signal for their downfall within twenty-four hours of the meeting of the Chamber . . . .[26]

Delcassé's determination to convince the British that he could accept no abject capitulation over Fashoda was reflected in the two French newspapers whose views consistently paralleled those of the Quai d'Orsay. On 5 October *Le Matin* headlined: " NO! THE ONLY RESPONSE WORTHY OF FRANCE." This emphatic " no," the editorial explained, was in response to any official demand that Marchand be recalled without prior negotiations and British concessions.[27] On 10 October the influential *Le Temps* praised Delcassé for his " *sang-froid* " in the negotiations with Britain, and concluded that just as *The Times* could promise Lord Salisbury the support of all Britain, so could *Le Temps* pledge Delcassé " *l'appui de toute la France unanime.* " [28]

The increasingly grave circumstances convinced Delcassé that he would have to make some move before he received Marchand's situation report, a document which was being hand-carried to Paris by Captain Baratier. On 3 October he brought the Fashoda question before his colleagues in the cabinet for a second hearing.[29] Delcassé undoubtedly reviewed the details of his meeting with Monson on 30 September, which he had now come to think of as a " historic day " during which he had used diplomatic tact to prevent war with Britain. He then went on to convince them that the recall of Marchand was the only way to avoid a pointless war, and that this action could be profitably traded for territorial concessions in the Bahr-el-Ghazal. On 4 October, Baron Courcel, who was on leave in Paris pending retirement, was sent to London

26. PRO, FO 78/5051, no. 491: Monson to Salisbury, 1 October 1898. See also Salisbury Papers, A/116, no. 47: Monson to Salisbury, 2 October 1898.

27. Arié, " L'Opinion publique en France," p. 350. The *Le Matin* article was translated in full and forwarded to London.

28. " Bulletin de l'étranger," *Le Temps*, 10 October 1898. Delcassé has heavily underlined his copy of this article, and it is probable that it was inspired by him. According to Robert de Billy, a member of Delcassé's *cabinet*, the French Foreign Minister often personally drafted items he wanted printed in those journals which were friendly to the government.

29. MAE, Lettres de Delcassé, 4 October 1898; and Sanderson, p. 344.

with a concrete French proposal—the first that had been offered. Courcel was instructed to tell Salisbury that France would recall Marchand if Britain would cede the whole region bounded by the Bahr-el-Arab, the Bahr-el-Ghazal, and the Upper Nile.[30]

Courcel first discussed the Fashoda question with Salisbury on 5 October. Rather than reveal the extent of French demands at this point, Courcel limited himself to saying that France was now quite willing to evacuate Fashoda in return for access to the navigable Nile system. An agreement might emerge, Courcel suggested, from a discussion of the geographical position to which Marchand might retire. On 5 October and then again on 12 October, Courcel requested " such a territorial delimitation as would place France upon the navigable portion of the Bahr-el-Ghazal, so that no frontier would intervene between her commerce and the Nile." Salisbury showed a willingness to make concessions along these lines and promised to bring them before his ministerial colleagues.[31]

Following the 12 October exchange, Courcel, perhaps encouraged by Salisbury's willingness to negotiate, wrote the British Prime Minister a private letter which implemented Delcassé's 4 October instructions by asserting France's claim not simply to territory on the Nile, but to the whole region bounded by the Bahr-el-Arab, the Bahr-el-Ghazal, and the Upper Nile. The extent of French demands took Salisbury by surprise, and the prospects for a negotiated settlement dimmed considerably.[32] During the last week of October Delcassé regretted that he had ever asked for so much and informed the British that any outlet on the Nile would be acceptable to France. By this time, however, the domestic crisis in France had entered a new phase which enormously complicated the tasks of diplomacy, and completely destroyed any chance that might have existed for a compromise solution over Fashoda.

III

On 13 September the excavation workers (*terrassiers*) of Paris, their numbers swelled because of projects underway for the Inter-

30. *DDF*, XIV, no. 163: Delcassé to Courcel, 4 October 1898.
31. PRO, FO 78/5051, no. 369: Salisbury to Monson, 12 October 1898; *DDF*, XIV, no. 414: Courcel to Delcassé, 6 October 1898; no. 433: same to same, 13 October 1898; Sanderson, pp. 346–47.
32. PRO, FO 78/5051, Courcel to Salisbury, 12 October 1898; Salisbury to Courcel, 13 October 1898.

national Exhibition of 1900, voted to strike. By 17 September, between 2,500 and 3,000 angry laborers were assembling daily at the Bourse centrale du travail to hear their leaders threaten a general strike of the entire working class unless their demands for wage hikes were met.[33] The call for a general strike evoked a widespread response; within three weeks numerous other construction workers, from carpenters to stone masons, had joined the *terrassiers*, and over 30,000 men were out of work.[34] On 6 October a Comité centrale de grève was formed to coordinate the strike effort and to expand further the massive protest.[35] The Parisian economy was rapidly grinding to a halt.

The strike quickly became intertwined with the politics of the Dreyfus affair. *L'Aurore* and *La Petite République* editorially supported the workers' demands for higher wages, donated substantial sums to the strikers' fund, and dispatched speakers to strike meetings.[36] This attempt to recruit the strikers for the revisionist cause was only partially successful. Although a majority of the working class may have been pro-Dreyfusard,[37] the primary motivation of the September–October 1898 strike was economic,[38] and on many occasions revisionist speakers were shouted down when they tried to introduce politics into meetings called to discuss the strike. Certain worker groups were anti-Dreyfusard and made no secret of their position.[39] Nevertheless, the nationalist right, with the exception of Henri de Rochefort and his followers, condemned the strike as part of the general Dreyfusard conspiracy

33. APP, Ba/107: Rapport quotidien, 17 September–11 October 1898.

34. APP, Ba/1396: Grève générale des terrassiers, renseignements généraux; and " Les grèves en France en 1898," *Bulletin de l'office du travail*, IX (June 1898), 516–17.

35. APP, Ba/107: Rapport quotidien, 7 October 1898.

36. APP, Ba/1397: Grève générale des terrassiers, souscritions et secours, mesures d'ordre, " Au Sujet de la distribution des secours entre ouvriers terrassiers," 6 October 1898. Also, *L'Aurore* and *La Petite République*, 17 September–20 October 1898. See especially " Pour les grévistes," *L'Aurore*, 15 October 1898.

37. Charles Péguy, " Notes politiques et sociales, l'affaire Dreyfus et la crise du parti socialiste," *Amitié Charles Péguy*, XLVI (1955), 15–22; LII (1956), 14–28; LIV (1956), 2–18. Péguy was one of the first writers to stress the class basis of the revisionist movement.

38. APP, Ba/1396: Grève générale des terrassiers, renseignements généraux, " Genèse de la grève," report of 16 September 1898.

39. APP, Ba/107: Rapport quotidien. On 21 September a revisionist speaker was interrupted when the assembled laborers began to chant in unison: " *Vive l'armée! A bas Dreyfus! A bas les juifs!* " Other incidents similar to this occurred between 20 September and 17 October.

to weaken the nation.[40] The response to the strike, therefore, further polarized the French political spectrum.

The Brisson cabinet was under severe strain. To the burden of dealing with the affair and Fashoda was now added a full-scale social crisis. Prime Minister Brisson, who devoted the bulk of his time and attention to immediate problems created by the affair, seemed unable to cope with either Fashoda or the spreading strike. Delcassé, therefore, turned more and more to President Faure for guidance and leadership.[41]

On 25 September Delcassé conferred with Faure at the President's Rambouillet estate. Delcassé saw in the Dreyfusard movement and the strike a general unleashing " of all anti-social elements against the army " and favored a " vigorous act of salutary energy " to restore order and confidence.[42] Faure, who like Delcassé saw the necessity for revision but was repelled by the tactics of the Dreyfusards, also favored a show of force in dealing with domestic disorder. After 25 September both men began to push for drastic measures to deal with a situation which was fast getting out of hand, and by the first week of October the views of the President and the Minister of Foreign Affairs were accepted as official government policy.[43]

The army ordered infantry troops from the provinces to Paris on 6 October. Within hours all of the construction sites of the capital were occupied. By the end of the week roughly 60,000 soldiers had moved into Paris and its banlieues.[44] At night campfires burned along the Seine and the Champs-Elysées. Army tents dotted the Champ de Mars. Paris took on the aspect of a city under siege.[45]

Despite the government's show of force, the strike continued to expand as union after union voted to join the growing protest

40. BN, n. a. fr. 13499: Mme. Dardenne, p. 48. See also *La Libre Parole*, 6 and 12 October 1898; Georges Thiébaud, " Les Coulisses de la grève," *Le Gaulois*, 9 October 1898; and Alphonse Humbert, " Autour des grèves," *L'Eclair*, 15 October 1898.

41. NPFF, LIX: " Affaires d'Angleterre," 7 November–30 December 1898. Also, *Souvenirs de Louis Le Gall*, pp. 204–9.

42. MAE, Lettres de Delcassé, 25 September and 6 October 1898.

43. *Souvenirs de Louis Le Gall*, p. 178.

44. Reinach, *Histoire de l'affaire Dreyfus*, p. 288.

45. The headlines of all the papers of Paris and London were concerned with the story of troops in Paris. The drawings in the October issues of *L'Illustration* present a vivid picture of the presence of troops in the capital. See also Alexandre Zévaès, " L'Etat de siège," *Le Socialiste*, 16 October 1898.

movement.[46] By 12 October over 43,000 Parisians were on strike. The magnitude of the social crisis was understandably disconcerting to the Brisson cabinet, and an even more intense current of alarm shocked government circles when on 12 October the Paris Prefecture reported that the National Railway Workers Union of France had scheduled a nationwide strike for 14 October.

In normal times a strike threat by this union would scarcely have disturbed the government. Most observers both within and outside the government were aware that the Railway Workers Union was among the weakest in France. Only in Paris could labor leaders claim to have unionized over thirty per cent of the railway employees. In the provinces there was even less union support. In Lyon, for example, only 200 out of 4,000 railway workers were union members, and of this 200, only 50 were actively engaged in union activities. In addition, many railway employees were members of the Fédération générale des chauffeurs et méchaniciens de France et d'Algerie, and this union opposed the strike.[47]

The government's reaction to the forthcoming strike was probably dictated by factors other than the strength of the railway workers union. By the first week of October both Delcassé and President Faure were fearful that at any moment the Fashoda crisis would erupt into war. Their alarm could only have increased when on 6 October they received an intelligence report based on first-hand observation stating that the British were engaged in extraordinary naval preparations.[48] On 12 October Minister of Marine Edouard Lockroy requested the Ministry of War to order regular infantry troops to the port cities of Cherbourg, Brest, and Toulon, and the following day the first contingent of what was soon to become a force of over 5,000 soldiers was moving by rail toward these coastal cities.[49] In these circumstances a nationwide railway

46. APP, Ba/107: Rapport quotidien, 4–16 October 1898. After 6 October non-construction workers joined the strike.

47. APP, Ba/1363: Grève des travailleurs des chemins de fer (declarée le 13 Octobre 1898). See also Le Petit Journal, 15 October 1898; and " Grèves avortées," Le Matin, 15 October 1898.

48. MG, Services des renseignements, carton 13: Angleterre, 1898–1901, no. 1519: " Préparatifs maritimes anglais," 6 October 1898.

49. Ministère de la Marine (MM), BB[81].903c, "Note relative aux mesures prises par le département de la marine . . . au sujet de la défense du littoral," prepared 28 January 1898.

strike was seen as a threat to the national security, and extraordinary measures went into effect.[50]

By 14 October, the day the strike was publicly proclaimed, the
Brisson cabinet had decided to use force to disrupt the strike at
its very inception. On the morning of that day, between 50 and
100 army troops occupied each of the major railway stations in
Paris and the provinces.[51] The rumor was already spreading that
massive and violent reprisals were planned, and the military occupation of the railway stations seemed to confirm this view. The
use of troops was producing an extremely dangerous reaction;
according to contemporary observers, something similar to the
" great fear " of the revolutionary period was sweeping France.[52]

The greatest fear was that of a military coup d'état. Mathieu
Dreyfus later recalled the atmosphere which reigned in Dreyfusard circles following the first influx of troops into Paris:

> What would be the result of contact between the soldiers
> and workers? A single word, a single cry, a single gesture,
> and a barrage of shots?
>
> We were extremely uneasy because we knew that the Gen-
> eral Staff desired disturbances in the streets. Grave trouble
> in the streets would justify the proclamation of a state of
> siege. And once the state of siege was decreed, all power
> would pass into the hands of the military . . . .
>
> A single word or the act of an *agent provocateur* would
> have sufficed to produce the explosion.[53]

These fears were at first confined to private discussions, but by
the second week of October *L'Aurore* and *La Petite République*
carried almost daily headline warnings of a *complot militaire*
designed to overthrow the government and arrest leading revisionist agitators.

The Sûreté générale was also concerned about the prospect of

50. The railway union leaders realized they would be charged with threatening
the national security, and included in their public propaganda pledges that they
would call off the strike if the government requested them to do so in the higher
interests of national defense. The government, however, chose never to discuss this
issue with the union. See APP, Ba/1363, for examples of the posters used.

51. " Les Mesures d'ordre," *Le Figaro*, 15 October 1898.

52. Reinach, *Histoire de l'affaire Dreyfus*, pp. 270–300; Zévaès, *L'Affaire Dreyfus* (Paris, 1931), pp. 135–51; Chapman, *Dreyfus Case*, p. 235.

53. BN, n. a. fr. 14379: Mathieu Dreyfus, Souvenirs sur l'affaire Dreyfus, p. 244.

a coup d'état. Early in October Sûreté agents began reporting that a coalition of the Ligue des patriotes, the Ligue antisémitique, the Orleanists, and top generals in the French army was planning drastic action to forestall complete revision of the Dreyfus case.[54] On 13 October another Sûreté agent submitted a report on the response of the strikers to the presence of troops in the streets of Paris:

> The revolutionary journals, by their articles and by other means at their disposal, endeavor to present this augmentation of the garrison as a serious provocation. The response is most disturbing . . . .
> One hears that an enormous nationalist and anti-Semitic demonstration is being prepared for 25 October when the Chamber reconvenes, and the rumor is spreading that the troops massed in Paris will serve to enforce rather than to prevent the actions of the nationalists.[55]

The nationalist press did little to allay the fears of the Dreyfusards and strikers concerning the projected demonstrations of 25 October. Drastic action, *La Libre Parole* repeatedly suggested, would be the order of the day, and a *La Patrie* article summed up the nationalist line in two ominous sentences: " The hour of decisions and solutions is approaching . . . . 25 October will fix the destiny of the French Republic." [56]

The Dreyfusards also became convinced that 25 October would mark a decisive confrontation in the history of the Third Republic. Jean Jaurès, who sincerely feared a coup, worked furiously to unite the forces of the left to face the nationalist challenge. On 16 October his work bore fruit when a Comité de vigilance comprising all the major socialist factions of France was formed, and when its leaders agreed to cooperate tactically with nonsocialist elements in defense of the Republic. A vast counterdemonstration was planned for the day the Chamber reconvened.[57]

The approaching confrontation between the opposed coalitions

---

54. AN, F⁷12717: Jean, " *La Libre Parole* et les Orléanistes," 4 October 1898; and Pierre, " La Revision de procès Dreyfus et l'armée," 6 October 1898.

55. AN, F⁷12717: Albert, " Ce qu'on dit des troupes à Paris dans les milieux grévistes et socialistes," 13 October 1898.

56. *La Libre Parole*, 14, 16, and 22 October; *La Patrie*, 19 October 1898.

57. APP, Ba/1620: Comité du vigilance du parti socialiste (fondé le 16 Octobre 1898 sous les auspices de *La Petite République*).

was further complicated by a division of opinion on foreign policy issues. The Dreyfusards, socialist as well as nonsocialist, were antimilitarist and anticolonialist in varying degrees. Many leading Dreyfusards were pacifists and internationalists. On the other side, opposition to pacifism and internationalism, and a belief that the army was the heart of the nation and the bedrock of its strength and security characterized the anti-Dreyfusard nationalists. The anti-Semitism of the nationalists was very largely a result of their belief that the Jews of France were agents of an international conspiracy to weaken the nation; the " treason " of Dreyfus was taken as confirmation of this view.[58] Given these general preconceptions, it should come as no surprise that the nationalists and the Dreyfusards did not exactly see eye to eye when it came to the concrete case of French policy in the Fashoda crisis.

The Dreyfusard press favored a soft line from the very beginning of the Fashoda crisis. The socialist journal *La Petite République* set the keynote. In a 21 September front-page article entitled " Vers le Nil," Maxence Roldes indicted the nationalists for their strong support of Marchand as well as for appealing to the " national interest " as a " magic formula " instead of presenting a rational explanation of French policy on the Nile. The views of the nationalists, Roldes continued, would " launch France into the most criminal of adventures ": war with Britain. The article closed with a clarion call to the socialists of both France and Britain to renounce the conflict in the Nile Valley as an unjust struggle between " two capitalist minorities." [59] On a less ideological note the nonsocialist journal *Le Siècle* condemned the entire Upper Nile project as " senseless " and demanded Marchand's immediate recall.[60] Although Clemenceau's *L'Aurore* was less dogmatic than either *La Petite République* or *Le Siècle*, there was never any doubt of the journal's opposition to colonial expansion and its advocacy of a conciliatory line toward Great Britain.[61]

All the journals of the right viciously attacked Dreyfusard

58. See the excellent articles of Raoul Girardet, " Pour une Introduction à l'histoire du nationalisme français," *Revue française de science politique*, VIII (1958), 503–28; and " L'Histoire du nationalisme français et ses problèmes," *Revue des travaux de l'académie des sciences morales et politiques*, III (1958), 112–31.

59. Maxence Roldes, " Vers le Nil," *La Petite République*, 21 September 1898.

60. Arié, " L'Opinion publique en France," p. 353.

61. Georges Clemenceau, " Meditations sur Fachoda," *L'Aurore*, 25 October 1898.

publicists for their " anti-patriotic " views. This was very largely because the nationalists were enchanted by Marchand's heroic exploits and the adventurous affirmation of national independence and strength which his mission embodied. *La Libre Parole*, *L'Autorité* and *Le Gaulois* were effusive in their praise of Marchand, and strongly deplored the fact that this " noble figure " and the cause of national prestige which he symbolized were endangered by internal quarrels resulting from Dreyfusard " agitators." *La Nouvelle Revue* neatly summed up the emotional tenor of the nationalist response to the Fashoda issue in a single sentence: " *Le Commandant Marchand est l'expression complète de notre race; il est notre porte-drapeau.*" [62]

Nationalist papers strongly opposed any concessions to the British and favored the retention of all of the territory which had been annexed to the French empire by Marchand. Thus, once Delcassé's scheme to recall Marchand in exchange for concessions became public knowledge during the first week of October, the Foreign Minister became the special object of nationalist wrath. Déroulède, writing in the 17 October issue of *La Patrie*, labeled Delcassé a " traitor " who had sold out completely to the " hereditary enemy." In his own journal *L'Intransigeant*, Rochefort argued that the Ministry of Foreign Affairs was a Dreyfusard hotbed, and that all French foreign policy was being manipulated by the international Dreyfusard movement.[63]

The strikers also were a target for nationalist spleen. The rumor spread that the primary contributors to the strike fund were the Jewish bankers of Britain, an idea which conformed very well to the nationalist view of the world. Unfortunately, this conspiratorial rumor was given credence by none other than the Minister of Commerce in the Brisson cabinet, Maruejouls. " We know," the minister told a group of businessmen, " that the strike leaders have at their disposal as much money as they want. We also know that this money is coming from England." *La Cloche*, the journal that reported these words, concluded by suggesting that the coincidence of the Fashoda crisis and the growing strike in France was far from accidental.[64]

As the 25 October demonstration approached, the nationalists

62. Arié, " L'Opinion publique en France," p. 350.
63. *Ibid.*, p. 352.
64. " D'où vient l'argent," *La Cloche*, 14 October 1898.

became more and more concerned about the Fashoda question. At a private planning session of the Ligue des patriotes on 21 October, Déroulède gravely warned his comrades that France was " on the eve of war with England," and that such an event was likely because the Brisson cabinet sought by any means at its disposal to " dismember France and deliver it over to the foreigner." In the minds of the anti-Dreyfusards, 25 October would give them a chance to protest against French policy in the Fashoda crisis as well as against revision of the Dreyfus case.[65]

The Paris Prefecture of Police was fully aware of the foreign policy dimension of the coming demonstrations and took this into consideration while planning the *mesures d'ordre* for the day. Special guards were stationed at the Ministry of Foreign Affairs, and increased police protection was ordered for the British embassy. In addition, a special plan was worked out to prevent any overt attack against either Brisson or Delcassé. Early on the morning of 25 October Brisson was secretly taken to the Quai d'Orsay. Then, as over 5,000 emotional demonstrators, the majority of them nationalist sympathizers, assembled in the Place de la Concorde, the Foreign Minister and the Prime Minister quietly walked with an armed guard out a back exit of the Quai d'Orsay and along the rue de l'Université to the back entrance of the Palais Bourbon.[66]

As he walked, Delcassé undoubtedly reflected on the words he had written three days before in reference to the growing criticism of his foreign policy: " justice is not of this world, at least not of the political world." That same day he predicted that " this week will certainly bring the denouement of the Anglo-French crisis," and in order to prepare for this eventuality, he at last issued the *Livre jaune* on Fashoda.[67] On 24 October he spent the entire day collecting his thoughts and arguments to meet effectively the avalanche of criticism he expected in the Chamber the following day.[68] All of this preparation was in vain. Soon after the session opened, Fashoda was momentarily forgotten in the confusion which accompanied Minister of War Chanoine's dramatic and

65. APP, Ba/1533: Manifestations à l'occasion de la rentrée des chambres (25 Octobre 1898), " Réunion privée de la ligue des patriotes (Salle Charras)," 21 October 1898.

66. *Ibid.*, " Manifestations, mesures d'ordre," 25 October 1898.

67. MAE, Lettres de Delcassé, 22 October 1898.

68. *Ibid.*, 24 October 1898.

unexpected resignation. General Chanoine's act precipitated the event which Delcassé had feared since the *faux Henry*: late on 25 October the Brisson cabinet was overthrown.

IV

The entire succession of dramatic events in France was being closely followed by the staff of the British embassy in Paris. "The existing condition of unrest and suspicion," Monson wrote on 16 October, "is interesting to England on account of the influence it may exercise upon the foreign relations of France." Just as in January 1898 when Monson was first required to deal with this problem, the rumor was again spreading that events were moving toward a military coup d'état which would be quickly followed by war with Britain. And, just as in January 1898, the cautious ambassador's first reaction was to discount such a possibility.[69] Not until 25 October did he alter his forecast.

Monson's initial views on the coup d'état rumors were in keeping with his entire approach to diplomacy. Since September he had made an effort to remain calm and to tone down as much as possible the generally tense atmosphere. By 21 October, however, even Monson was becoming exasperated and frightened by the onrush of events. The Dreyfus affair, and especially the "ostentatious criticisms and disquisitions of the most influential London newspapers" on the affair, Monson complained, were rendering "the task of diplomacy, so far as [it] is concerned with keeping the peace, more difficult than ever." He added ominously that those who had formerly believed that the entire Fashoda question could be handled amicably now viewed the situation "in a very different light." [70]

On 25 October Monson completely abandoned his previous caution. Soon after the Chamber reconvened, news reached him of the dramatic events within the Palais Bourbon and of the massive demonstrations in the Place de la Concorde. Monson immediately telegraphed London that Chanoine's resignation was "an act of treachery which looks like the first step to a military coup d'état." [71] He then drafted a long dispatch which placed the

69. PRO, FO 27/3397, no. 524: Monson to Salisbury, 16 October 1898. Also see above, pp. 65–69.
70. *Ibid.*, no. 533: Monson to Salisbury, 21 October 1898.
71. PRO, FO 27/3400, no. 186: Monson to Salisbury, 25 October 1898.

domestic situation in a larger context. The events of the day, Monson wrote, presaged the " probable outbreak of a crisis " which might well lead to the " advent of a military government or of a nominally civilian government in the hands of the military party." If this occurred, he suggested, the new government would certainly abandon the conciliatory foreign policy which had been pursued to date by the Brisson cabinet, and this would gravely endanger both the " internal and external tranquility." [72]

Colonel Dawson, the British military attaché in Paris, had long believed that the French internal situation seriously threatened the " external tranquility." As early as 14 October he had submitted to Monson a secret report which argued that a group of dissident generals was plotting to seize power at the first available opportunity. Once the generals had taken over, Dawson believed, there would be war with Britain.[73] The situation was potentially explosive, his reports to London stressed, because " five French army corps were under orders to prepare for the invasion of England . . . ," and numerous French admirals were bragging that " England need not count on a speedy termination of the war . . . ." [74]

On 16 October Sir John Charles Ardagh, the director of British Military Intelligence, ordered Dawson to London to brief the upper echelons of the British army and navy on the situation in France. So much concern was provoked that Ardagh instructed Dawson to make the Channel crossing each evening, report personally on what he had learned the previous day in Paris, and then return immediately for more firsthand information. During each of his nightly encounters with British military authorities, a sleepy and haggard Dawson reported on the deteriorating domestic situation in France and warned his superiors to prepare for the worst.[75]

Dawson's warnings, which were initially discounted, began to be taken seriously during the last week of October. The British

72. PRO, FO 27/3397, no. 546: Monson to Salisbury, 25 October 1898. See also Salisbury Papers, A/116, no. 55: Monson to Salisbury, 25 October 1898.

73. PRO, FO 27/3397, no. 522: Monson to Salisbury, 14 October 1898. Enclosing Dawson to Monson, secret report no. 42. And Salisbury Papers, A/116, no. 53: Monson to Salisbury, 16 October 1898.

74. Dawson, *Soldier-Diplomat*, pp. 241 44. On Dawson's early role in the affair, see above, pp. 66–67.

75. *Ibid.*

Admiralty ordered the Reserve Squadron put in readiness on 24
October. On 26 October war orders for the Home, Mediterranean,
and Channel Fleets were drafted, and the First Sea Lord called
for the immediate concentration of the Home Fleet. The Admiralty, however, could take no further steps without the formal
approval of the government.[76]

The Salisbury cabinet met in a crisis-charged atmosphere on
28 October to deal with the Fashoda emergency. War sentiment
within Great Britain, which had been feeding on chauvinistic
political speeches and exaggerated press accounts since September,
had reached alarming proportions.[77] Added to this domestic pressure within Britain was the unsettling picture of the French internal situation which had slowly become accepted in official
British circles. Dawson's views seemed conclusively confirmed
when on 25 October, Monson, one of Britain's most respected
diplomats, went so far as to forecast a " government of generals
[which] might even welcome war with England if they could in
this way stave off the ' revision ' of the Dreyfus case . . . ." [78] Seen
from London, France appeared to be on the eve of civil war—
weak, but potentially warlike and aggressive. Most members of
the cabinet, whose views were shaped at least in part by the situation in France as interpreted by Monson and Dawson, favored
immediate and drastic action.[79]

Lord Salisbury sought to resist the pressures of the moment and
presented to the cabinet a French compromise solution to the crisis
which Courcel had communicated to him on 26 October.[80] This
proposal made no mention of the large territorial concessions demanded earlier and offered a " spontaneous " recall of Marchand
if Salisbury would " spontaneously " offer negotiations which
would give France a commercial outlet on the Nile. This compromise solution was received very coldly by Salisbury's colleagues,
who, as Lord Esher noted at the time, " seemed to take the view

76. A. J. Marder, *The Anatomy of British Sea Power* (New York, 1940),
pp. 320–26.

77. M. Hugodot, " L'Opinion publique anglaise et l'affaire de Fachoda," *Revue
d'histoire des colonies*, XLIV (1956), 113–37.

78. Sanderson, p. 349. Also see Chapman, *The Dreyfus Case*, pp. 236–38.

79. *Journals and Letters of Reginald, Viscount Esher*, ed. M. V. Brett, I
(London, 1934), 221–22. Hereafter cited as *Journals and Letters of Esher*. For a
discussion of this point, see below, pp. 128–30.

80. CCO, Salisbury Papers, A/89: Cabinet Memoranda, no. 83; *DDF*, XIV,
no. 455: Courcel to Delcassé, 26 September 1898.

that the row would have to come and that it might as well come now as later."[81] Minister of Colonies Chamberlain and First Lord of the Admiralty Goshen, both of whom were apprehensive about Salisbury's determination to stand firm, went even further and probably pressed for an immediate preventive war against France.[82] As a minimum, most members of the cabinet seem to have favored an ultimatum to France coupled with a military show of force.[83] Salisbury, who was in an extremely difficult position, managed to block effectively the sending of an explicit ultimatum, but nonetheless accommodated himself to the spirit of the meeting and reluctantly allowed the Admiralty to put the navy on a war footing.[84] On 28 October the war orders which had been drafted two days earlier were signaled to the Mediterranean Fleet, and on 29 October the Channel Fleet was ordered to Gibraltar.[85]

V

The British naval mobilization faced Delcassé, who possessed only the uncertain status of a *ministre démissionaire* at this critical moment, with his most difficult decision since taking office in June 1898. Since the beginning of the crisis Delcassé had counted on his own diplomatic ability to extract from the British, and particularly from Lord Salisbury, concessions which he could present to the French public as a diplomatic success. Delcassé's confidence was severely shaken by the mobilization of the British fleet and by the dispatch which he received from London on 28 October, however. Courcel reported that according to Salisbury Britain could allow neither compromise nor negotiation as long as the French flag flew at Fashoda, and that there could be no British promise of concessions even if Marchand were recalled. Courcel commented that Salisbury was under pressure from his colleagues to remain adamant, and that this was the final word of the British.[86] The following day the French ambassador advised Del-

81. *Journals and Letters of Esher*, pp. 221–22.
82. J. L. Garvin, *The Life of Joseph Chamberlain*, IV (London, 1934), 228–31; Langer, *Diplomacy of Imperialism*, p. 561.
83. Sanderson, p. 350.
84. Salisbury's reluctance is underlined in *Journals and Letters of Esher*, pp. 221–22.
85. Marder, *Anatomy of British Sea Power*, pp. 320–26.
86. DDF, XIV, no. 459: Courcel to Delcassé, 28 October 1898.

cassé that France should withdraw from Fashoda at once while it was still possible to do so " *avec honneur et la tête haute.*" [87]

Courcel's advice came at a time when domestic French opposition to a capitulation was mounting to a climax. On 26 October Marchand's envoy, Baratier, arrived in Paris with the situation report which the cabinet had requested in late September.[88] The elaborate reception arranged for Baratier at the Gare de Lyon clearly demonstrated the degree to which the older colonial groups were now supported by anti-Dreyfusard nationalist formations. Monteil and other representatives of the Comité were there, as well as the colonial group's spokesman, Etienne. In addition to these colonial stalwarts, the returning hero was greeted by the nationalist deputy Marcel Herbert and a massive demonstration of 3,000 to 7,000 cheering participants which had been organized by the Ligue des patriotes. Etienne's welcoming speech was accompanied by chants of the crowd which alternated between a nationalist chorus of " *Vive l'armée* " and a colonialist refrain of " *Nous resterons à Fachoda.*" [89]

Baratier, elated and optimistic following the Gare de Lyon reception, met with Delcassé on 27 and 28 October. On both occasions he endeavored to persuade the Foreign Minister that France should stand firm against British demands. He countered Kitchener's description of the dismal condition of the French force at Fashoda with a much more optimistic assessment: the mission was well-provisioned and well-armed, Baratier stressed, and could remain in place until reinforcements reached the area. When Delcassé refused to accept this view, and even went so far as to speak of evacuation routes, Baratier resolved to appeal his case to the leaders of the French colonial movement.[90]

Baratier's plea did not go unanswered. On 28 October *La Dépêche Coloniale* demanded war rather than submit to the humiliation of recalling Marchand. The following day most of the French newspapers carried a manifesto drawn up by Etienne and signed by a number of deputies in the colonial group which protested the conclusion of any Franco-British settlement without prior debate in the Chamber.[91] Also, on 29 October the Ministry

87. *DDF*, XIV, no. 465: Courcel to Delcassé, 29 October 1898.
88. See above, p. 97.
89. Baratier, *Souvenirs*, pp. 206–13; Albéric Darthèze, " Le Capitaine Baratier à Paris," *L'Aurore,* 27 October 1898; and *Le Temps,* 27 October 1898.
90. Baratier, *Souvenirs*, pp. 206–13.
91. PRO, FO 78/5052, no. 566: Monson to Salisbury, 30 October 1898.

of Colonies, in an act which aimed at justifying long years of support for the Upper Nile project, forwarded to the Quai d'Orsay Baratier's report entitled " Renseignements sur la situation de la mission à Fachoda " with the suggestion that it be used to gain concessions from the British before recalling Marchand.[92]

Under this barrage of demands Delcassé's conduct of French policy became most erratic. On 27 October when Monson met with the French Foreign Minister, he found him agitated and close to breaking under the strain of the situation. Delcassé, who had remained calm during all previous encounters, emotionally declared that he would resign rather than allow France to be humiliated.[93] And by 29 October Delcassé was grasping at straws when he instructed Courcel to propose yet another compromise solution to the crisis. On the following day, however, he countermanded these instructions by writing that it was " useless " to continue along these lines.[94] Finally, on 31 October Courcel learned from Geoffray, who was then in Paris, that Delcassé was considering a disconcerting plan which probably called on Marchand ostensibly to withdraw from Fashoda and then link up with the Ethiopians and other reinforcement missions so that at a more opportune moment France could effectively challenge Kitchener's Anglo-Egyptian force.[95]

Courcel, who was convinced that Marchand should immediately be recalled in the interest of peace, dispatched a frantic message to Geoffray.

> This seems to me to be pure folly, dangerous folly. Act [now], I beg you. Everything depends on you. Straighten out these visionaries. Do not allow them to have their way.

92. MC, Afrique III, 33: Affaire de Fachoda, 2 Octobre–30 Octobre 1898, no. 11: Ministry of Colonies to Delcassé, 29 October 1898.

93. *British Documents on the Origins of the War*, I, no. 221: Monson to Salisbury, 28 October 1898.

94. *DDF*, XIV, no. 464: Delcassé to Courcel, 29 October 1898; no. 469: same to same, 30 October 1898.

95. The exact details of this plan are uncertain because Geoffray's letter to Courcel has disappeared. According to Sanderson (p. 351), " it is clear from Courcel's reply that Delcassé was under pressure, doubtless from the Parliamentary colonial group and its fellow travellers, to refuse the evacuation of Fashoda and damn the consequences." Courcel's 1 November dispatch (p. 116, n. 97), however, suggests that Courcel's concern was not that Delcassé would " refuse the evacuation of Fashoda and damn the consequences," but rather that Marchand would be allowed to link up with the Ethiopians and that this might lead to war.

Return to the rue de Constantine [another address for the Ministry of Foreign Affairs]. If you cannot see and enlighten M. D[elcassé], at least see N[isard] .... If necessary I may ask you to go on my behalf to the Elysée ....[96]

The following day he warned Delcassé in no uncertain terms that if the Marchand mission linked up with any Ethiopian force, " *c'est naturellement la guerre avec l'Angleterre.*" [97]

Geoffray, following Courcel's suggestion, seems to have thought it necessary to go directly to the Elysée. If he did, he found President Faure just as disturbed as Courcel about Delcassé's refusal to recall Marchand without further maneuvering. Although Faure had been one of the founding members of the Comité, he now condemned those " irresponsible men who are called colonialists " for leading France to adopt a policy so ambitious that it " completely exceeded our naval power." For Faure the mobilization of the British navy decided the issue. " During the ministerial crisis," he later wrote, " the gravity of the situation became extremely alarming; we feared an immediate attack. I pressed Delcassé to order the evacuation of Fashoda ...." But not until the President agreed to accept full responsibility for this decision did Delcassé give his reluctant consent. This paved the way for Delcassé's inclusion in the new Dupuy cabinet; Trouillot, who remained opposed to recall, was excluded from the new combination.[98] On 1 November the cabinet was formed; on 3 November it voted for Marchand's recall.

---

96. *DDF*, XIV, no. 473: Courcel to Geoffray, 31 October 1898.
97. *Ibid.*, no. 476: Courcel to Delcassé, 1 November 1898.
98. NPFF, LV: " Crise ministérielle du 25 Octobre," November 1898; LIX: " Affaires d'Angleterre," 7 November–30 December 1898.

PART III

DOMESTIC AND INTERNATIONAL POLITICS:
AN ANALYSIS

CHAPTER VIII

DOMESTIC SOURCES OF THE FASHODA DEFEAT, I

Marchand's recall signified much more than the failure of a French foreign policy initiative. As early as 7 September Delcassé concluded that the Upper Nile project, with its goal of forcing the British to reopen the Egyptian question, was doomed to failure. He did not realize, however, that his more modest aim of gaining token concessions from the British would also be denied him, and that by the end of October France would be faced with a choice between a naval war and an abject capitulation. In these circumstances the French decision to order Marchand's recall was a major diplomatic defeat; the decision also represented, in the minds of contemporary Frenchmen, a national humiliation.

Even before the Fashoda crisis had run its course, the question of individual responsibility for the approaching defeat was posed. " Opinion will be severe," Delcassé wrote on 24 October, " on those who [launched the Marchand mission]." [1] Gabriel Hanotaux, who was already being criticised as an author of the crisis, embarked on a private campaign to dissociate himself from the goals of the Marchand mission. On 25 October he told British journalist Wilfrid Blunt that " nobody in France knew where Fashoda was, or cared three straws about the Marchand mission." " He even considered the Egyptian question itself," Blunt later recalled, " one of small importance to France. As for the Bahr el gazal [sic], it was ' a country inhabited by monkeys and by black men worse than monkeys.' " [2]

After the fall of the Brisson cabinet Hanotaux sought to prepare the way for his return to office by discrediting Delcassé. He tried to convince President Faure that Delcassé had ineptly handled French foreign affairs since taking office in June, and was therefore responsible for the gravity of the Fashoda crisis. Hanotaux

1. MAE, Lettres de Delcassé, 24 October 1898.
2. Wilfrid S. Blunt, *My Diaries* (London, 1932), p. 303.

119

argued that if he had remained at the Quai d'Orsay he would have avoided the crisis by concluding an agreement with Germany, and by opening discussions with Great Britain at an earlier date. President Faure dismissed Hanotaux's pleadings as an attempt to justify himself " after the events." " The truth is," Faure later concluded, " that Hanotaux would have done no better than Delcassé given the circumstances." [3]

II

Delcassé's performance during the Fashoda crisis must be judged in terms of both his diplomatic goals and those circumstances which limited his freedom to implement these goals during September and October 1898.

Delcassé's early diplomatic aims have long been the subject of scholarly dispute. According to Charles W. Porter and other students of the problem, Delcassé was determined to bring Britain into an entente with France and Russia as early as June 1898 when he became Minister of Foreign Affairs.[4] No one disputes that at some point between 1898 and 1902 Delcassé chose to pursue the course of rapprochement with Britain which eventually led to the Triple Entente. But as Pierre Renouvin wrote in 1954, " the great difficulty is to determine when Delcassé really established this program. It is certain that this program was established in 1902, but it is not at all certain that it existed in June 1898." [5] In 1966, after examining the Papiers Delcassé for the first time, Renouvin reaffirmed his belief that this question remained unresolved.[6]

There is little in Delcassé's early career to suggest that he would ever come to be an advocate of an accord with Great Britain. In

3. NPFF, LIX: " Affaires d'Angleterre," 7 November–30 December 1898.

4. Porter argues that Delcassé favored the Anglo-French entente even in 1889, and makes this a primary theme of his study, *The Career of Théophile Delcassé*; see especially pp. 49–51. The following argue that Delcassé favored this course from June 1898 forward: Georges Reynald, *La Diplomatie française: L'oeuvre de M. Delcassé* (Paris, 1915), p. 22; René Pinon, *France et Angleterre* (Paris, 1913), pp. 117–18; Albéric Neton, *Delcassé* (Paris, 1952), pp. 201–33; Andrew, *Théophile Delcassé*, p. 91.

5. Renouvin, *La Politique extérieure de Théophile Delcassé*, pp. 8, 30–34 for a discussion of the problem.

6. Renouvin, " L'Orientation de l'alliance franco-russe en 1900–1901," *Revue d'histoire diplomatique*, LXXX (1966), 193–204. Renouvin had access only to the Papiers Delcassé; the Lettres de Delcassé were probably not deposited at the time of his research.

fact, there was a time when he favored an anti-British line and would have welcomed a Franco-British crisis over Egypt. In 1882, soon after the British occupied Cairo, Delcassé published a polemical attack against Foreign Minister Jules Ferry criticizing him for not defending " the rights of France in Egypt," and for " temporizing, conceding, deferring " rather than " deciding and acting." [7] As we have seen, when Delcassé became head of France's colonial department in 1893, he lost little time in deciding to reopen the Egyptian question, and in acting to implement the Monteil mission and later the Liotard mission.[8] Although both of these initiatives were undertaken before British policy was made unmistakably clear in the Grey Declaration of 1895, they nonetheless constituted an anti-British line.

Had Delcassé altered his earlier views and become a proponent of Franco-British rapprochement when he became head of the Quai d'Orsay on the eve of the Fashoda crisis? The evidence which is usually cited as proof of Delcassé's early intention to come to an accommodation with Britain is not entirely convincing. Delcassé's own testimony given in a 1908 speech before the Chamber affirmed that from the very beginning of his tenure as Minister of Foreign Affairs he had been in favor of an entente with Britain.[9] During the Fashoda crisis itself Delcassé told the British ambassador on several occasions that he sincerely desired closer ties with Great Britain.[10] But the 1908 speech, which was delivered in response to domestic criticism long after the Entente Cordiale was a reality, served the contemporary political situation and had the benefit of hindsight; and the statements made to Monson during the crisis could be dismissed as a pragmatic expedient of the moment, a tactical move to gain British sympathy.[11]

More conclusive evidence on Delcassé's early motives is now available. A letter written on 6 October 1898 includes the following revealing statement:

7. Delcassé, *Alerte! Où allons-nous?* (Paris, 1882), p. 8.
8. See above, pp. 24–32.
9. *Journal officiel*, 24 January 1908.
10. Langer, *Diplomacy of Imperialism*, pp. 555–56. The documents cited by Langer and others are in *British Documents on the Origins of the War*, I, nos. 188–91, 196, 198.
11. Marlin K. Farmer, " The Foreign Policy of M. Théophile Delcassé " (Ph. D. dissertation, Ohio State University, 1937). Farmer's criticism of the Porter thesis gives an excellent account of the context of Delcassé's 1908 speech.

I hope that they [the British] realized that the desire of
an entente with England, which I had very freely expressed
from the beginning of my term of office, arose not from a
feeling of weakness, but from a general political idea (*une
idée politique générale*) . . . .[12]

We have little reason to doubt that this statement represents
Delcassé's goals quite accurately. The views were expressed privately long before Delcassé could be certain that his " *idée politique
générale* " would ever be realized. Thus it cannot be dismissed as
either a product of hindsight or a tactical move to gain British
concessions.

There remains the possibility that Delcassé abandoned these
views after the French capitulation of 4 November 1898.[13] He
was certainly under growing pressure at home to take an anti-
British line. Nationalists like Maurras, Déroulède, Cassagnac,
Drumont, and Rochefort argued that the Dreyfus crisis was instigated by Great Britain in order to weaken France, and joined with
the Comité in demanding that France align herself with Germany
against Great Britain.[14] " If Germany is an object of hatred,"
Cassagnac explained, " it is for a definite past which can be effaced.
But England's hatred against us is inextinguishable, England is
the enemy of yesterday, tomorrow, and forever." [15] Thus, under
the shock of the Fashoda crisis, French nationalists made a sharp
about-face, and Britain replaced Germany as *l'ennemie par
excellence.*

Delcassé was wounded as deeply as any nationalist by the Fashoda defeat. In November he retreated into what Monson called
a kind of " funk " and Salisbury labeled a " sulk." [16] In December Monson thought that Delcassé was " impressed to a certain
extent by the echoes of [the colonial party's] outcries," and was

12. MAE, Lettres de Delcassé, 7 October 1898.
13. See Langer, *Diplomacy of Imperialism*, pp. 567–70.
14. Charles Maurras, *Au Signe de flore* (Paris, 1931), pp. 58–59; anon. [Robert
de Caix], " La Leçon de Fachoda," *BCAF*, VIII (November 1898), 358–62; and
anon., " La France et l'Angleterre après Fachoda," *BCAF*, VIII (December 1898),
391. Monson's interpretation of the colonial " party's " advocacy of a rapprochement with Germany is in Salisbury Papers, A/116, no. 65: Monson to Salisbury,
13 November 1898.
15. Quoted in *The Times* (London), 14 November 1898. Cited by Langer,
Diplomacy of Imperialism, p. 566.
16. CCO, Salisbury Papers, A/116, no. 68: Monson to Salisbury, 25 November
1898; A/117, no. 30: Salisbury to Monson, 15 November 1898.

considering a Triple Alliance of France, Russia, and Germany against Great Britain.[17]

Monson's assessment came at a time when Franco-British tension was still very high. The British fleet remained in a state of alert, and reports continued to reach Delcassé indicating that the tension might result in open conflict.[18] Delcassé seems to have taken these reports seriously enough to consider it necessary to warn Britain subtly that if a military conflict did ensue he might try to gain German assistance. Thus, Delcassé's hints to Monson were probably a tactical response to what he considered a dangerous situation.

Delcassé's long-range strategy, however, remained unchanged. Toward the end of December 1898 Maurice Paléologue recorded the following exchange in his diary.

" I see," he [Delcassé] said to me, " that you have understood my position quite correctly. Henceforth, the Dreyfus Affair must remain on the juridical plane. In any case I will not allow it to impede my political action. I did not come to the Quai d'Orsay to remain inactive; I have an enormous task to fulfill and I intend to do it well! "

Then he spoke to me of his negotiations with England which are well underway. The evacuation of Fashoda will soon be no more than a sad memory. At the same time he said that he was delighted by his personal relations with Muraviev.

At this point I recounted to him what the Emperor's uncle, Grand Duke Wladimir, told me recently at a dinner at the home of Countess Talleyrand: " I hope I live long enough to see England near death: that's the ardent prayer I address daily to God! "

Delcassé reacted immediately and, like someone in a trance [replied]: " What an error! What blindness! . . . For both Russia and France, England is a rival and a competitor whose conduct is often harsh and extremely disagreeable. But Eng-

17. *Ibid.*, no. 72: Monson to Salisbury, 9 December 1898. "Delcassé," Monson wrote, " has always had relations, more or less intimate, with the Colonial Party . . . . " Monson seems to have included both the colonial group and the Comité in his general category, the " Colonial Party."

18. See especially, MAE, Papiers Delcassé, III, Cambon to Delcassé, 12 December 1898.

land is not an enemy, and above all, England is not *the Enemy* . . . . Ah! My dear Paléologue, if only Russia, England and France could conclude an alliance against Germany!" [19]

Delcassé, therefore, was entirely unsympathetic to the colonialist-nationalist campaign to brand Britain as the eternal enemy of France, and retained, despite the Fashoda defeat, his " general political idea" of bringing Britain into the Franco-Russian alliance.

This conclusion leaves us with a still more difficult question: what led Delcassé to abandon his early anti-British views and to adopt a policy of rapprochement with Britain? " Somewhere," writes Sanderson, " there must be a link between the aggressive filibustering Delcassé of 1893, eager to strike England at her most vulnerable point, and the sober Delcassé of 1898 who, although a badly frightened man, was also quite genuinely anxious for an all-round improvement in Anglo-French relations." After posing the question, however, Sanderson limits himself to the " speculation" that Delcassé's change of view may have begun as early as 1894 when he chose as Monteil's successor the civilian Liotard, a " conscientious but rather pedestrian administrator . . . [and] not the man for an epic operation in the Peters-Stanley style." [20]

Sanderson's rather disappointing explanation of Delcassé's change of mind is a result of the near absence of evidence on Delcassé's attitudes and opinions in the years between January 1895, when he ceased to be Minister of Colonies, and June 1898, when he became Minister of Foreign Affairs. In December 1894 Delcassé remained a strong advocate of a forward policy on the Nile, and the choice of Liotard to accomplish his goals does not alter this conclusion. In June 1898, however, he envisioned the " general political idea" of an entente with Britain. These facts are clear, but in the absence of direct evidence we can only speculate as to the reasons for Delcassé's changed outlook.

Delcassé's activities and speeches while out of office suggest a possible explanation. During this period he became deeply interested in the French navy, and, like many of his European

19. Paléologue, *Journal de l'affaire Dreyfus*, p. 154. Emphasis in the original.
20. Sanderson, p. 207.

contemporaries, in the effects of naval power on history.[21] By 1898 he had become known as an expert on naval matters, and many observers expected him to be named Minister of Marine in the Brisson cabinet rather than Minister of Foreign Affairs.[22] Delcassé was undoubtedly aware, therefore, that despite increased French spending in the naval budget, the gap between France and Britain opened wider each year. In 1893–94 France's total naval budget was a little over 245 million francs; Britain's was higher, but still amounted to only 383 million francs. There was an even smaller difference between amounts expended for new construction: France, 68 million; Britain, 74 million. By 1898–99, however, France had fallen far behind Britain. France's total naval budget, 289 million francs, was less than half that of Britain, 635 million francs. And although France had expanded the amount allocated to new construction to almost 86 million francs, Britain's soaring expenditures in this field were now 172 million, more than twice the French amount.[23] Delcassé must also have been aware that German naval expenditures had increased sharply since 1894, and that in October 1897 William II accepted the Tirpitz program for significantly augmenting the strength of the German navy.[24]

Delcassé was probably sobered both by Germany's serious entrance into the naval race and by France's inability to keep pace with Great Britain. He may have come to the conclusion that in the long run French national interests—especially the goal of regaining Alsace-Lorraine—would best be served by abandoning policies which placed France at odds with the strongest naval power in the world of the 1890's.[25] The above argument, which is offered in the absence of any direct evidence, provides us with at least one reason for the shift in Delcassé's attitudes which occurred between

21. Porter, *Career of Théophile Delcassé*, p. 104; Andrew, *Théophile Delcassé*, pp. 88–97. Langer describes the interest in naval power which swept Europe in the 1890's, *Diplomacy of Imperialism*, pp. 418–28.

22. See above, p. 77. Years later, Delcassé became Minister of Marine (1911–13). See Philippe Masson, "Delcassé, Ministre de la Marine" (Thèse de Diplôme d'Etudes Supérieures d'Histoire, Sorbonne, n. d.).

23. MM, BB7, Dossier 157: Marines comparées, [Budget report, 6 May 1899].

24. Langer, *Diplomacy of Imperialism*, pp. 425, 433–34.

25. Delcassé felt so strongly about Alsace-Lorraine that he forbade his children to utter the names of the lost provinces in his presence, and on the eve of the Fashoda crisis he declared that "la France se souvient toujours—c'est sa principale raison d'être." See MAE, Lettres de Delcassé, Mme. Noguès' Preface, p. ii; Papiers Delcassé, XI: Russie, 1898–1914, no. 2: [Conversation with Prince Ouroussoff], 31 August 1898.

1895 and 1898. Another reason may be simply that Delcassé's views were modified by the experience of what he once spoke of as the " stultifying air they breathe at the Quai d'Orsay." [26] In 1893 and 1894 Delcassé could advocate African adventures without seriously considering the European ramifications of such initiatives; in 1898 he was charged with judging any external initiative against the balance sheet of national interests. This kind of national accounting probably played a large role in moderating Delcassé's once strident views.

Delcassé's reasons for shifting from an anti- to a pro-British outlook are not entirely clear. Whatever his motives for this shift were, the basic conclusion remains unchanged: Delcassé very probably desired an accommodation with Great Britain when he became Minister of Foreign Affairs in June 1898. By this time, however, Marchand had already reached Fashoda, and the stage was set for a confrontation with Britain which Delcassé did not desire, but which he could have prevented only by ordering Marchand's retreat before tension had begun to increase in September 1898. Instead of taking action immediately after assuming office, however, Delcassé occupied himself with the glory and fanfare of mediating the Spanish-American War.[27] By not acting, Delcassé prepared the way for the international crisis which occurred in September and October 1898.

III

Delcassé's freedom of action between 1 September and 4 November 1898 was sharply prescribed by domestic factors. His primary diplomatic goal from beginning to end was to convince the British that he sincerely desired a general accommodation; his secondary goal was to gain concessions from Britain before recalling Marchand. Delcassé's primary goal probably resulted from his assessment of the international political scene; his secondary aim was almost certainly dictated by his interpretation of the changing internal situation.

The fear of a ministerial crisis haunted Delcassé from the time he learned of the *faux Henry*. His immediate response to the dramatic re-emergence of the affair was to attempt to convince his colleagues that revision was inevitable and that by their taking the

26. MAE, *Lettres de Delcassé*, 18 July 1893.
27. See above, pp. 78–79.

lead in this process the cabinet could be saved. By 7 September he was momentarily encouraged to believe that the Dreyfus case would soon be relegated to the juridical plane, that public agitation would be stemmed, and that the position of the cabinet would therefore be secured.[28] Thus, when Delcassé opened the diplomatic dialogue with Monson on 7 September, he was free to express his views without worrying about domestic repercussions. Monson came away from this first encounter convinced that Delcassé had dismissed Marchand as a mere " emissary of civilization," and that all would soon be arranged amicably—unless, Monson added, the French domestic situation changed.[29]

Delcassé, also, wanted everything to be arranged amicably. On 7 September he completely and formally abandoned the goal of reopening the Egyptian question with all of its explosive possibilities, and belatedly ordered the Ministry of Colonies to instruct Marchand to stop his advance short of Fashoda. Before the colonial department took any action, however, Delcassé learned on 25 September that Marchand had already reached Fashoda. Although he still desired a settlement with Britain, he believed that if he recalled Marchand the Brisson cabinet would be overturned.

Delcassé's renewed fear of a ministerial crisis was linked to the changed domestic situation in France. The Brisson cabinet had taken the first step toward revision on 17 September, but, unexpectedly, this move increased public agitation; the strength of the cabinet, rather than being shored up, was undermined. Given these circumstances, Delcassé decided not to recall Marchand. He had come to believe that the domestic attacks against the cabinet could be offset by gaining some concessions over Fashoda and presenting them to the French public as a foreign policy success.[30] Thus, Delcassé prolonged the tension between France and Britain by holding out for concessions, and what might have been only a minor incident took another step toward becoming a major crisis.[31]

Lord Salisbury, like Delcassé, began the Fashoda negotiations with the desire for an amicable settlement. Although he was at

28. MAE, Lettres de Delcassé, 7 September 1898. Also see above, pp. 81–82.
29. See above, p. 86.
30. See above, pp. 85, 90–93, 99–100.
31. Robinson and Gallagher make the same point in *Africa and the Victorians*, pp. 374–75.

no time prepared to make any serious concessions to France, he did not rule out the offering of some token to keep the representative of one of the Great Powers from being completely humiliated.[32] It seems that he ordered Kitchener to make specific recommendations for a " frontier line granting large concessions to France, that might from a military point of view . . . be given them without injuring our position in this part of Africa." [33] The boundary which was recommended by Kitchener included some of the Nile basin, and many areas which " were subject to Egyptian rule before the Mahdi revolt." [34] Salisbury, who was not anxious to commit Britain to " liabilities which would be burning subjects of penitent reflection to the Treasuries both of England and of Egypt," [35] would have been happy to accept Kitchener's suggestion; and it almost goes without saying that, at least by the end of October, the Kitchener boundary would have been eagerly accepted by Delcassé. Thus, if Salisbury had had his way, these concessions could have been offered to France, and the Fashoda negotiations could have been concluded without escalating into a military confrontation.

Salisbury was under strong domestic pressure to offer absolutely no concessions, however. Following Trouillot's disclosure on 26 September, demands increased within Britain for a harder line against France.[36] Salisbury responded by publishing a diplomatic *Blue Book* on the crisis and by rejecting Delcassé's request for large concessions in the Upper Nile. By the time Delcassé had scaled down his demands to a point Salisbury may well have accepted, the domestic crisis in France had destroyed any chance which might have existed for a compromise settlement.

In October the domestic situation in France entered a new and most critical phase; a tremor of fear swept Europe. On 29 September Delcassé received from Rome a report which argued that many European observers " believe in the possibility of a war provoked by the French military party." [37] As the domestic situation

32. See above, pp. 92, 100–101, 112–13.
33. PRO, FO 78/5051, Kitchener to Cromer, 8 October 1898.
34. *Ibid.*
35. CCO, Salisbury Papers, A/119, no. 30: Salisbury to Monson, 15 November 1898.
36. See above, pp. 98–99, 100–101.
37. MAE, Papiers Delcassé, XII: Italie, Blondel (Rome) to Delcassé, 29 September 1898.

worsened and troops were used extensively to quiet widespread labor disturbances, the fear of a military coup followed by war increased. When French domestic tension reached its climax on 25 October, the Italian authorities ordered the ports of Genoa and La Spezia put in a " state of defense." [38] The German Emperor was also alarmed. On 29 October he urgently wired his ambassador in Paris requesting the latter's opinion on whether or not " a coup d'état or a revolution " was probable. In the margin of Münster's cautious reply of 30 October the Emperor wrote: " A coup d'état, therefore, is in sight . . . I have informed Gossler and Schlieffen." [39] Similar prevalent fears in Brussels were reported to London.[40] Thus, in Italy, Germany, Belgium, and probably in other capitals, the French domestic situation provoked serious concern.

It is also probable that the French crisis played a role in the decisions of British policy makers. Robinson and Gallagher have gone so far as to say that Monson's 25 October dispatch which reported the real possibility of a coup " undoubtedly " led the Salisbury cabinet to authorize naval preparations.[41] Although the evidence presently available does not justify such a sweeping judgment, it is reasonable to argue that the very gravity of the situation in France made the reports of Dawson and Monson much more readily believable than they might have been in more normal times, and that the Dawson-Monson reporting probably played a substantial role in the late October decisions of the British government.[42]

Salisbury was opposed to the drastic measures of late October. Although he reluctantly allowed naval preparations to proceed, he seems to have vetoed a proposal to couple mobilization with an ultimatum demanding the immediate recall of Marchand. In addition, he privately tried to be as conciliatory as possible by communicating an " unofficial " memorandum to Courcel stating that French claims would be given unprejudiced consideration after

38. PRO, FO 146/3531, no. 394: Currie (Rome) to Salisbury, 26 October 1898.

39. Baumont, *Aux Sources de l'affaire*, p. 227. Gossler was Minister of War; Schlieffen, Chief of the General Staff.

40. PRO, FO 46/3531, no. 382: Plunkett (Brussels) to Salisbury, 16 October 1898; no. 410: same to same, 30 October 1898.

41. Robinson and Gallagher, *Africa and the Victorians*, p. 375.

42. See above, pp. 105–6, 110–12.

Marchand's recall. Salisbury then authorized an official of the Foreign Ministry to give Courcel a written statement confirming that Britain had at no time formally demanded the evacuation of Fashoda.[43] Thus, from beginning to end, Lord Salisbury attempted to remain conciliatory and to adjust the Fashoda difficulty without humiliating France.

IV

The policy-maker, argues Edgar S. Furniss, " may reach conclusions as to foreign policy based on his interpretation of the internal setting which his reading of the international setting would lead him to discard . . . ." [44] This certainly seems to have been the case in the Fashoda crisis. Delcassé's interpretation of the international setting led him to favor an entente with Britain and to discard the policy of reopening the Egyptian question which he had supported during his early career. But his assessment of the internal situation led him to fear a ministerial crisis and, in an effort to prevent the fall of the cabinet, to demand concessions from Britain. These demands prolonged tension between France and Britain well into October. In late October the unstable internal situation in France seems to have created serious doubts in the minds of British policy-makers, and the opinions of moderates like Salisbury were swept aside when the decision was made to mobilize the British navy. My detailed investigation of the Dreyfus-Fashoda conjuncture, therefore, confirms an insight offered by Robinson and Gallagher: " The Fashoda incident became the Fashoda crisis because of the condition of French politics." [45]

Once events had reached the crisis stage, the diplomatic question of Marchand's recall was posed in terms of naval power. The French navy was vastly inferior both in over-all tonnage and in organization. The Ministry of Marine could count only 565,388 tons in the French armed fleet, as opposed to 1,074,266 tons of better-equipped British warships. Even if the tonnage of France's ally Russia were entered into the calculation, Britain was still far

43. *DDF*, XIV, no. 465: Courcel to Delcassé, 29 October 1898 (enclosing the unofficial memo by Salisbury, 27 October 1898); *British Documents on the Origins of the War*, I, no. 220: Sanderson to Courcel, 28 October 1898. Sir Thomas Sanderson was permanent Undersecretary of State for Foreign Affairs.
44. Edgar S. Furniss, *The Office of the Premier in French Foreign Policy-Making: An Application of Decision-making Analysis* (Princeton, 1954), pp. 58–59.
45. Robinson and Gallagher, *Africa and the Victorians*, p. 374.

superior.[46] In addition, both the French and the Russian navies were in no condition to sustain a major conflict, and this fact was recognized by both the Ministry of Marine and Delcassé himself.[47]

Should we, therefore, conclude with Sanderson that "as a motive for the French surrender Dreyfus counted for nothing beside the glaring naval inferiority of France," or should we follow Renouvin in listing French naval weakness as a secondary consideration when compared to the impact of the Dreyfus affair?[48] The two interpretations are reconcilable. The domestic situation created by the affair acted to force events to the crisis stage; but once the British navy was mobilized, naval power tipped the balance and France capitulated. Thus, the combined influence of domestic politics and French naval inferiority produced the Fashoda defeat.

46. MM, BB[7], dossier 157: Marines comparées, "Tableau faisant connaitre le déplacement total de la flotte moderne des 8 grand puissances maritimes . . . ," prepared June 1899. Combined Russian and French tonnage in 1898 was just over 825,000 tons.

47. R. Masson, "La Marine française lors de la crise de Fachoda" (Thèse de Diplôme d'Etudes Supérieures d'Histoire, Sorbonne, 1955), p. 17. MAE, Lettres de Delcassé, 22 October 1898. Also see the candid account by the Minister of Marine in 1898, Edouard Lockroy, La Défence navale (Paris, 1900), especially pp. 1–22.

48. Sanderson, p. 361; Renouvin, La Politique extérieure de la Troisième République, p. 277. Arié also stresses the importance of the affair, "L'Opinion publique en France," p. 364.

CHAPTER IX

DOMESTIC SOURCES OF THE FASHODA DEFEAT, II

In September 1898 Kitchener quipped that French policy, as embodied in the Marchand mission, was " more worthy of Opéra-Bouffe than the outcome of the maturely considered plans of a great Government." [1] This is a harsh judgment and fails to take into consideration that when the Marchand mission was launched there was no 20,000-man Anglo-Egyptian army in the Egyptian Sudan. Kitchener's criticism, however, is partially justified: French policy toward the Upper Nile and Egypt between 1893 and 1898 was certainly not the outcome of maturely considered plans of the French government.

The Upper Nile project, from its inception to its tragic conclusion, had only a narrow base of support. At no time between 1893, when the Monteil mission became the archetype of all future French action projects on the Upper Nile, and 1898, when Marchand at last reached Fashoda, did the policy of forcing the British to reopen the Egyptian question by establishing a French presence on the Upper Nile obtain the unreserved approval of the Ministry of Foreign Affairs. Neither were all the implications of the Marchand mission ever fully understood and debated by the French cabinet.

II

As tension increased between the Ministry of Colonies and the Ministry of Foreign Affairs in mid-September 1898, Trouillot sought to transfer responsibility for the emergent crisis from his department to the Quai d'Orsay.[2] " You must be aware," he wrote Delcassé, " that the French operation in the Egyptian Sudan has been only a manifestation of our general [foreign] policy." [3]

1. PRO, FO 141/333, no. 153: Rodd to Salisbury, 29 September 1898 (enclosing Kitchener to Rodd, 21 September 1898). Cited by Sanderson, p. 338.
2. On tension between the two ministries, see above, pp. 96–97.
3. *DDF*, XIV, no. 352: Trouillot to Delcassé, 15 September 1898.

Trouillot's assertion completely distorts the history of French policy toward the Upper Nile. The impulse for a forward policy on the Nile came not from diplomatic decision-makers at the Ministry of Foreign Affairs charged with the formulation of France's general foreign policy, but rather from domestic political forces acting in concert with the colonial department.

The idea of launching a French mission toward the Upper Nile was first conceived by a small pressure group, the Comité de l'Afrique française. The Comité gained access to government circles by establishing a close relationship with the colonial department, rather than by directly approaching the tradition-bound Ministry of Foreign Affairs. Acting through the Pavillon de Flore, the Comité eventually came to wield considerable influence on the formulation of French colonial policy in general, and Upper Nile policy in particular. A major step toward this success came in 1893 when Théophile Delcassé, a key member of the Comité's parliamentary ally, the colonial group, became Undersecretary of State for Colonies.[4]

Delcassé's attitudes and personal ambitions coincided with the goals of the Comité. The young deputy, following what seems to be a law of bureaucratic politics, was anxious for his department to play a more important role in the conduct of French external policy. Thus, in 1893 when the President of the Comité, Prince d'Arenberg, first suggested sending a mission to the Upper Nile, Delcassé added his own ideas to those of the pressure group and energetically began to campaign for an acceptance of what became the Monteil mission. He bypassed the Ministry of Foreign Affairs completely and secretly planned the Monteil mission with Prince d'Arenberg and the President of the Republic, Carnot. Before Monteil ever reached Africa, however, Delcassé fell from office and the project foundered.

When Delcassé returned to power in May 1894, the colonial department had been raised to the rank of a full ministry, and the new Minister of Colonies was more determined than ever that his organization increase its influence. The new Minister of Foreign Affairs, Gabriel Hanotaux, was equally resolved that the Quai d'Orsay retain its established position as arbiter of French foreign affairs. Hanotaux opposed a forward policy on the Nile because it contradicted his department's diplomatic goal of im-

4. See above, pp. 19–24.

proving relations with Great Britain, and because it ran counter to a traditional French policy which recognized the " integrity of the Ottoman Empire." [5]

The first clash between Delcassé and Hanotaux came in the summer of 1894 when Great Britain and the Congo State announced the conclusion of an agreement to partition the Nile Valley between them. The colonial group immediately raised a chorus of protest in the Chamber and demanded vigorous action. The Ministry of Colonies also urged some positive initiative and proposed a revival of the Monteil mission. Hanotaux, who strongly favored an accommodation with the British and had initiated diplomatic negotiations to accomplish this goal, was in an extremely difficult position. In a speech before the Chamber he protested against the Anglo-Congolese agreement, and clearly implied that he intended to launch a new Upper Nile mission, which indeed he did. Behind the scenes and against Delcassé's protests, however, Hanotaux issued new instructions which sharply limited the aims of the revived Monteil mission. The Ministry of Foreign Affairs, therefore, had won the first round.[6]

Delcassé immediately began to plan another Upper Nile mission and soon decided that it should be headed by the civilian Liotard. In order to obtain approval for this initiative, the Minister of Colonies tried to undermine Hanotaux's personal position in the Dupuy cabinet. This was an especially difficult undertaking because the members of the cabinet were, like most French parliamentarians, both uninterested and uninformed in foreign policy, and generally accepted the views of the Minister of Foreign Affairs in the area of his competence. Delcassé was fortuitously aided in his task, however, because Hanotaux made himself extremely unpopular with his colleagues by opposing the indictment of Captain Alfred Dreyfus, a man whom most ministers believed was guilty of treason. At a cabinet meeting held on 17 November 1894, less than three weeks after Hanotaux was outvoted on the Dreyfus question, Delcassé was able to convince a majority of ministers present to vote against Hanotaux and in favor of the Liotard mission. The Minister of Colonies had won a clear victory.[7]

5. See above, p. 27.
6. See above, pp. 27–29.
7. See above, pp. 29–32.

In January 1895 Delcassé was replaced by Chautemps, and a short period of reduced interdepartmental tension ensued. The situation was further improved when in the spring of 1895 it was learned that Liotard had come to a near-standstill far short of Fashoda. Hanotaux used this opportunity to renew his efforts toward a peaceful settlement of the Nile problem. Despite the fact that the British had hardened their stand on the Upper Nile following the Grey Declaration, these negotiations might have succeeded if domestic politics had not intervened at this juncture and disrupted the continuity of French foreign policy.

In the summer of 1895 one of the frequent ministerial crises which beset the Third Republic brought about the fall of Hanotaux and the Ribot cabinet.[8] Leon Bourgeois, the premier-designate, found the task of constructing a new cabinet extremely difficult because of the widespread lack of sustained interest in foreign affairs which reigned in the Chamber. Unable to find deputies who were both experienced in foreign affairs and willing to assume ministerial responsibility, Bourgeois turned first to the diplomatic corps, where he was rebuffed, and then, as a last resort, to two politically inexperienced academicians, Berthelot and Guieysse.

The Comité, acting through high-level career officials at the Ministry of Colonies like Roume and Archinard, seized the opportunity presented by the presence of new and inexperienced leaders at the Quai d'Orsay and the Pavillon de Flore to press for an immediate acceptance of the Marchand mission. This campaign, which was mounted in an atmosphere of the utmost urgency, succeeded on 30 November 1895 in extracting from a confused and incompetent Berthelot the only official written approval for the Marchand mission which the Ministry of Foreign Affairs ever issued.[9]

Berthelot's 30 November dispatch contained a number of significant reservations. He explicitly stated that the Marchand mission should be strictly nonmilitary and should not engage in an " act of occupation." In addition, Berthelot gave no approval for any act which would reopen the Egyptian question. " Whatever he thought he was approving," concludes Sanderson, " it cannot have entered his mind that he was launching an enterprise which three years later was to seem a deliberate challenge to British

8. The Ribot cabinet fell on the issue of a strike in Carmaux.
9. See above, pp. 36–44.

hegemony throughout the Nile Valley." [10]   But surprisingly
enough, it was on the basis of Berthelot's 30 November approval
that the permanent officials of the Pavillon de Flore were able to
convince one Minister of Colonies, Lebon, that the Marchand
mission was undertaken " only at the request of French diplomacy," and another, Trouillot, that the operation was a manifestation of France's " general [foreign] policy."

Hanotaux returned to office in 1896 and remained in power
until June 1898. He therefore had ample time to assert his
authority, enforce the restrictions placed on the Marchand mission
by Berthelot, and thereby halt an initiative which he correctly
believed to be counter to what remained his diplomatic goal, an
accommodation with Great Britain. Yet even when the substantial
British military build-up in Egypt began in January 1898 and the
African balance of power tipped decisively in Britain's favor,
Hanotaux made no move to call off the Marchand mission.

Hanotaux's failure to act was a direct result of domestic political
factors. His position in the cabinet was weak because he was not
a deputy and therefore wielded no influence in the Chamber. To
recall or restrict the Marchand mission would have led directly
to an open confrontation with the Ministry of Colonies and to an
outcry from members of the colonial group in the Chamber. In
these circumstances, Hanotaux decided simply to let the Pavillon
de Flore follow what amounted to an independent course. As
Monson remarked, between 1896 and 1898 the Minister of Foreign
Affairs was " more of a mouthpiece than a free agent " in African
affairs.[11]

The Ministry of Colonies itself was not under the firm control
of a responsible minister. André Lebon, who headed the colonial
department between 1896 and 1898, was more politically experienced than Guieysse, but was strongly influenced by his African
experts, Archinard, and Roume's successor, Binger. These two
men seem to have presented the history of the Marchand mission
to Lebon in such a way as to convince him that the project was
undertaken " only at the request of French diplomacy," and that
French policy would be reduced to " incoherence " if " each ministerial crisis involved a change of plans." [12]

10. Sanderson, p. 276.
11. See above, pp. 31–32, 74–75.
12. André Lebon, " La Mission Marchand et le cabinet Méline," *Revue des
deux mondes*, CLVIII (March 1900), p. 276.

With both Hanotaux and Lebon offering no effective opposition, Archinard and Binger swept aside the restrictions which had been placed on Marchand by Berthelot. The original aims of the Marchand mission, which had been clouded and confused in 1896, re-emerged in November 1897 when Marchand received orders to throw off the cloak of secrecy which had characterized the first phase of his mission and advance openly toward Fashoda with the intention of provoking a confrontation with Britain.

There is some doubt concerning the degree to which the Méline cabinet as a whole was aware of the final goals of the Marchand mission. In the fall of 1897 the cabinet voted to overrule Hanotaux and to approve a Ministry of Colonies project, already well underway, designed to reinforce Marchand by using Ethiopian troops.[13] This would tend to indicate that the cabinet approved of the Marchand mission and its goals. On the other hand, President Faure has written that as late as June 1898 the prospect of reopening the Egyptian question after Marchand arrived at Fashoda had never been raised at a meeting of the Méline cabinet.[14] In the absence of any direct record of the cabinet proceedings of the Third Republic, a definite conclusion on this important question is difficult. It is possible that Lebon presented both the Marchand and Ethiopian missions as operations with limited territorial aims in the Upper Nile basin, and that the cabinet was never informed of the scheme's Egyptian implications. If either Lebon or Hanotaux had ever discussed the Egyptian question at a cabinet meeting when Faure was absent, a member of the cabinet would probably have brought such a sensitive matter to the attention of the President, a man known for his interest in foreign affairs. Faure's testimony, therefore, is probably accurate. It seems likely that the most crucial policy questions raised by the Marchand mission were never debated by the cabinet, and that the central goal of the project never obtained the cabinet's approval.[15]

III

The above review of French policy formulation suggests that the only determined and dedicated supporters of the Upper Nile operations of the 1890's were the leaders of a small but influential

13. See above, pp. 53–54.
14. Faure, " Fachoda," p. 30.
15. Andrew, *Théophile Delcassé*, p. 45.

pressure group, the Comité de l'Afrique française; certain members of a small loosely organized band of deputies, the colonial group; an ambitious young minister, Delcassé; and a handful of career officials in a single government department, the Ministry of Colonies. This minority movement, using " methods which can only be described as conspiratorial," [16] managed to launch an adventure which brought France to the very brink of war with Great Britain. The history of French Upper Nile policy, therefore, might well be seen as confirmation of Nizan's thesis in *La Conspiration*: " Little chances and little men manufacture great events." [17]

The above conclusion, however, leaves a more important question unanswered: what factors made it possible for a minority movement to launch an operation whose goals were never fully approved by the cabinet and which ran counter to the established policy of the responsible department charged with the conduct of French foreign affairs?

Backers of a forward policy on the Upper Nile succeeded in large measure because of structural weaknesses in the governmental system of the Third Republic. The first of these was the absence of a strong executive who could direct and coordinate French external policy, and the resulting dispersal of foreign policy authority into the hands of competing governmental departments. A second defect, ministerial instability, often interrupted the continuity of foreign policy, reduced the authority of responsible ministers, and increased the power of permanent career officials in the formulation of policy. These two defects combined to weaken the Ministry of Foreign Affairs and to make the Third Republic " a happy hunting ground for the activities [of pressure groups]." [18]

Contemporary Frenchmen were aware of these structural weaknesses. Both President Faure and Delcassé deplored the instability of the Third Republic and were in favor of strengthening the

16. Sanderson, p. 389.
17. Quoted by Sanderson, p. 389.
18. Philip Williams, *Politics in Post-War France* (London, 1958), p. 328. Williams also notes, speaking of the Fourth Republic, that where governmental authority is weak, " pressure politics flourish "; and, in another formulation of the same point: " Public morality is low where authority is diffused," p. 327. These insights are more than demonstrated by the history of French Upper Nile policy.

office of President of the Republic.[19] Neither of these men, however, ever offered an explanation of the problem as explicit and systematic as that of Christian Schéfer, a French political scientist and astute contemporary observer of Third Republic politics. After a lifetime devoted primarily to the study of French colonial expansion, Schéfer came to the following conclusions:

> We have already observed that at the time the Marchand mission was launched there was a certain lack of cohesion between diverse ministerial departments. Now this is an organic vice . . . . Internal and external affairs are interdependent and consequently ought to be under the control of a single directorship (*direction*). This kind of higher control was sometimes asserted during the history of the Third Republic, but only very rarely.

Schéfer then went on to attribute this lack of central direction in foreign affairs to the institutional structure of the Third Republic as it had evolved by the 1890's. The parliamentary republic, he argued, provided neither a chief of state nor a president of the Council of Ministers who had the necessary strength " to coordinate the projects of diverse ministries . . . ." [20] Schéfer's conclusions stand the test of time, and provide a useful insight into the relationship between domestic and international politics under the Third Republic.

IV

This case study was undertaken with the goal of determining the degree to which domestic politics influenced French policy in Africa in the last decade of the nineteenth century. The general conclusion should now be clear: from the inception of the Upper

19. CDFF, Faure to Montebello (St. Petersburg), 20 May 1898; and Charles Braibant in his introduction to *Souvenirs de Louis Le Gall*. For Delcassé's views on this question, see MAE, Lettres de Delcassé, Mme. Noguès' Preface, p. ix, and Delcassé to M. Nordheim, 13 February 1895; also A. Cambarieu, *Sept Ans à l'Elysée* (Paris, 1932), pp. 228–29, 286–87.

20. Christian Schéfer, *D'une Guerre à l'autre. Essai sur la politique extérieure de la Troisième République (1871–1917)* (Paris, 1920), pp. 227–28. Schéfer also published a number of excellent and insightful studies on the role of the Ministry of Marine in early nineteenth-century French colonial expansion, including *La Politique coloniale de la monarchie de juillot* (Paris, 1928). Very similar problems beset the Fourth Republic; see Furniss, *Weaknesses in French Foreign Policy-Making* (Princeton, 1954).

Nile project to its culmination in the Fashoda defeat, French foreign policy was decisively shaped by domestic political factors, and was often at odds with France's general diplomatic goals as defined by the Quai d'Orsay. More case studies are necessary before historians can conclude what I suspect will come to be an accepted judgment: foreign policy was not, even in the golden age of nineteenth-century cabinet diplomacy, "based upon changeless national and imperial necessities," and the distinction between the Old Diplomacy and the New Diplomacy, which forms the basis for so much discussion, is probably not so sharp as many old diplomatists would have it.[21]

21. Harold Nicolson, *Diplomacy*, 2nd ed. (London, 1950), p. 10.

BIBLIOGRAPHY AND COMMENTARY ON SOURCES

In an address at the University of Berlin in 1874, Theodor Mommsen asserted that "every thinking man generally is a seeker after sources and a pragmatic historian." This statement suggests the method used in researching my study: once the problems were posed, I sought pragmatically for sources which illuminated them. In defining the problems I was strongly influenced by J. H. Hexter's devastating attack on the "tunnel" approach to history in his *Reappraisals in History* (New York, 1961). Pierre Renouvin and Jean-Baptiste Duroselle's *Introduction à l'histoire des relations internationales* (Paris, 1964) provided valuable insights and a general orientation. More specifically, the concepts of internal setting and external setting developed in Richard C. Snyder, H. W. Bruck, and Burton Sapin's *Foreign Policy Decision-Making: An Approach to the Study of International Politics* (New York, 1962) suggested both the design of my research project and a systematic framework for organizing the source materials.

Listed below are only those documents and published works that have a direct bearing on the themes of this monograph. A much more comprehensive bibliography on the origins of French policy toward the Upper Nile and the Fashoda crisis is in G. N. Sanderson's *England, Europe and the Upper Nile* (Edinburgh, 1965), though his traditional diplomatic approach leads him to overlook some important sources. On the Dreyfus affair, see Paul Désachy, *Bibliographie de l'affaire Dreyfus* (Paris, 1905) and "Bibliographie sommaire de l'affaire Dreyfus depuis 1924," *Cahiers naturalistes*, III (1957), 354–56.

In the interest of brevity, I have given only the dossier or carton numbers for the unpublished sources. The titles of each dossier, as well as a more detailed description of all sources, may be found in my doctoral dissertation, "The Dreyfus Affair and Fashoda: A Study of the Interaction of Domestic and International Politics, 1893–1898," (University of California, Berkeley, 1968).

UNPUBLISHED PRIMARY SOURCES

1. FRANCE: THE INTERNAL SETTING

a. Archives de la Préfecture de Police, Département de la Seine

Beginning at the time of the revolutionary epoch, the Paris Prefecture became a highly centralized apparatus charged not only with law enforcement, but also with the collection and production of information on all aspects of domestic political activity in the Department of the Seine. A network of police agents spanned Paris, and during times of crisis the Prefecture could survey in great detail the changing political geography of the capital.

During the fall of 1898, reports on a variety of aspects of the Dreyfus-Fashoda conjuncture inundated the Prefecture. On the basis of these reports the Directorate of General Intelligence (Renseignements généraux) prepared a Rapport quotidien which summarized the number, size, and theme of all public meetings and demonstrations. Renseignements généraux also prepared dossiers on specific problems: especially revealing are the forty-nine cartons of reports on the strike which paralyzed Paris in September and October 1898 and the collection entitled Manifestations à l'occasion de la rentrée des Chambres, 25 Octobre 1898.

Ba/104–7, 653, 1338, 1363, 1396, 1397, 1406, 1533, 1620.

b. Archives Nationales

The private papers of certain members of the Marchand mission are now available: Monteil (66AP), Baratier (99AP), and Mangin (149AP). The Monteil papers are an important source for the political origins of the first Fashoda expedition; the Mangin and Baratier papers are rich in details on the march of the Marchand mission through Africa, but much of this material may also be found in the Afrique III 32–36 and Missions 42–44 at the colonial archives.

53AP: Papiers de Sallintin, Conseiller de la cassation concernant le procès Dreyfus includes the testimonies of Hanotaux and Casimir-Périer on the Dreyfus affair and its diplomatic implications.

Insight into the political dimension of the Dreyfus affair may be found in the F^7 Police générale series. Although the following dossiers are not as helpful as the Prefecture archives, they do contain valuable information.

$F^7$12449–51, 12717, 12870, 12882.

c. Bibliothèque de l'Institut

Fonds Auguste Terrier (1873–1932): 5891–92, 5894–5911, 5930, 5938.
Papiers de Berthelot (3929–3962).

d. Bibliothèque Nationale

N. a. fr. 13497–500: Mme. Henriette Dardenne. L'Affaire Dreyfus, crise de conscience nationale. This typewritten manuscript contains an extremely detailed account of the politics of the affair as seen from the right.

N. a. fr. 14379: Mathieu Dreyfus. Souvenirs sur l'affaire Dreyfus. This is especially useful for attitudes of the Dreyfusard milieu toward the rumored *complot militaire* of October 1898.

N. a. fr. 24327: Eugène Etienne. Correspondance, 1887–1921.

e. Private Collection

The private papers of former President Félix Faure are still in the possession of his grandson, M. François Berge. The collection, which has been edited by M. Berge, is divided into two categories:

Correspondance diplomatique de Félix Faure.
Notes personnelles de Félix Faure, 1894–1899.

2. France: The External Setting and Interdepartmental Politics

a. Ministère des Affaires Etrangères

Papiers Delcassé (25 volumes): I-VI, IX, X-XIV.

In addition to these volumes, there are six cartons of the Papiers Delcassé which have not been edited or bound. Cartons 14 and 15, Dossiers personnels, contain fragmentary information on Delcassé's domestic politics. Carton 16, Dossiers de presse (1898–1899), contains press clippings and the daily Résumé de la presse étrangère and Résumé de la presse française which the Foreign Minister's staff prepared for him. Cartons 17–20 are Dossiers de presse for 1899–1905.

Lettres de Delcassé à sa femme, à sa fille, à quelques amis, 1885–1923.

This small volume is not formally included in the Papiers Delcassé. It was edited by Delcassé's daughter, the late Mme. Noguès, and passages relating to personal and family matters have been excluded. The personal reflections of Mme. Noguès on the life of her father are included as a preface, and are of value. This small volume is a much greater contribution than the entire Papiers Delcassé.

Papiers Gabriel Hanotaux (23 volumes): II, IX, XI.

Diplomatic Correspondence

The *nouvelle série* of the French diplomatic papers for the period after 1897 is classified by country. They are then divided into volumes on Politique intérieure and Politique étrangère, an implicit commentary on the increasing importance of domestic politics during this period. The entire *nouvelle série*, unfortunately, is very poorly indexed and inventoried, and the various volumes contain no explanation of the principle of selection which guided their construction.

The Grande Bretagne collection contains most of the relevant material, but scattered pieces of important evidence were also found in the other collections listed below, especially Allemagne and Egypte.

Grande Bretagne

Politique intérieure: NS 1.
Politique étrangère: NS 8, 9, 11, 12, 28, 29.

Allemagne

Politique intérieure: NS 14.
Politique étrangère: NS 15, 26, 27, 53–59, 60, 63.

Egypte

   Politique intérieure: NS 1, 7, 8.
   Politique étrangère: NS 7, 19, 20, 30, 31.

Russie

   Politique intérieure: NS 1, 15.
   Politique étrangère: NS 16, 17, 34.

  b. Ministère des Colonies

Both the Direction politique et commerciale, Bureau de l'Afrique and the Direction de la défense, Bureau militaire kept records of the various Upper Nile missions. Bureau de l'Afrique records are classed as Afrique III, and include communications between the colonial department and the Ministry of Foreign Affairs. The Bureau militaire records are classed simply as Missions, followed by a number.

Afrique III 19, 32–36.
Mission 40, 42, 43.

  c. Ministère de la Guerre

Etat-Major de l'Armée, Deuxième Bureau: I-III, XIII.

  d. Ministère de la Marine

No *inventaire* on the holdings of the Marine archives is available to researchers. An unpublished thesis, Renée Masson, " La Marine française lors de la crise de Fachoda " (Thèse de Diplôme d'Etudes Supérieures d'Histoire, Sorbonne, 1955), served as an introductory guide to BB[7] 50, 157; BB[8]1, 903.

3. GREAT BRITAIN

  a. Foreign Office Papers in the Public Record Office, London

FO 27 (France), 1898–99: 3393, 3397–3400, 3455.
FO 146 (France: Embassy Archives), 1898: 3530, 3531.
FO 78 (Turkey: Egypt): 5051, 5052.

  b. Private Papers at the Public Record Office, London

There exist numerous collections of private papers of persons in or near the British Foreign Office during the Fashoda crisis. Of these, the Kitchener Papers (PRO 30/57) and the Cromer Papers (FO 633) offer some insight into the local crisis in Africa in 1898, but otherwise are not very helpful. Much more interesting are the Ardagh Papers (PRO 30/40); Major General Sir Charles Ardagh was Director of British Military Intelligence in 1898.

  c. The Salisbury Papers at Christ Church, Oxford

Of the 140 bound volumes of the series A correspondence, the following are relevant:
A/83, 84, 89, 92, 93, 96, 111, 113, 116, 117, 119.

PUBLISHED PRIMARY SOURCES

1. DIPLOMATIC CORRESPONDENCE: OFFICIAL PUBLISHED COLLECTIONS

British Documents on the Origins of the War, 1898–1914, ed. G. P. Gooch and H. W. V. Temperley. London, 1927 f.
Documents diplomatiques français (1871–1914). First series. Paris, 1929 f.

2. OFFICIAL PUBLICATIONS

a. Diplomatic

Egypt No. 2 (1898) C.–9054: Correspondence with the French Government respecting the Valley of the Upper Nile.
Egypt No. 3 (1898) C.–9055: Further Correspondence respecting the Valley of the Upper Nile.
Documents diplomatiques: affaires du Haut-Nil et du Bahr-el-Ghazal, 1897–1898.

b. Other

Annuaire de l'armée, 1898–1899.
Annuaire de la marine, 1898–1899.
Annuaire statistique de la ville de Paris, 1898.
Bulletin de l'office du travail, 1890–1900.
Bulletin du Ministère de l'Intérieure, 1898–1899.
Journal officiel, chambre des députés, débats parlementaires, 1893–1900.

3. THE PRESS AND CONTEMPORARY JOURNALS, PAMPHLETS, AND BOOKS

a. The Daily Press of France and Britain

The press has been used for two purposes: 1) to document the day-to-day course of events, and 2) to reconstruct the attitudes of the principal domestic political groups toward foreign policy. *Le Temps* and *The Times* have proved best for tracing the course of events. I have systematically examined *La Petite République* and *L'Aurore* for the views of the Dreyfusard left, socialist and nonsocialist. *La Libre Parole* was used to discover the attitudes of the anti-Dreyfusard right. Beyond this direct investigation, two studies of the press have proved helpful:
Arié, Rachael. " L'Opinion publique en France et l'affaire de Fachoda." *Revue d'histoire des colonies*, XLI (1954), 329–67. This is a detailed analysis of all the major Parisian and provincial dailies, and it is especially helpful because it concerns itself with the effects of the Dreyfus affair on the Fashoda crisis.
Hugodot, M. " L'Opinion publique anglaise et l'affaire de Fachoda." *Revue d'histoire des colonies*, XLIV (1956), 113–37.

b. The *Bulletin du Comité de l'Afrique française*

The *Bulletin* has been systematically studied for the period between January 1891, when the first issue appeared, and December 1898. The first few pages of each *Bulletin* present information on the activities and composition of the Comité.

4. THE CORRESPONDENCE, MEMOIRS, AND RETROSPECTIVE HISTORIES OF CONTEMPORARY PARTICIPANTS AND OBSERVERS

The volume of published correspondence, memoirs, and retrospective histories dealing with the origins of French policy toward the Upper Nile is a measure of the passionate tide of charges and countercharges which followed in the wake of the Fashoda debacle. Of these, the *Souvenirs* of Monteil, although tendentious, are important. Marchand's statements give his version of events, and are an explicit rebuttal to the views expressed in the books by Hanotaux and Lebon.

On other aspects of our problem, the memoirs of Colonel Dawson are an important, if neglected, source. And the Paléologue *Journal*, though it was probably altered after the events for dramatic effect, still contains valuable insights into the atmosphere created by the Dreyfus affair at the Quai d'Orsay and in the Section de Statistique.

a. France

Alis, Harry [Hippolyte Percher]. *A la Conquête du Tchad*. Paris, 1891.

Baratier, Aristide-E.-A. *Souvenirs de la mission Marchand, III Fachoda*. Paris, 1941.

Braibant, Charles, ed. *Félix Faure à l'Elysée* (*Souvenirs de Louis Le Gall*). Paris, 1963. Louis Le Gall was Félix Faure's *chef du cabinet*.

Brisson, Henri. *Souvenirs: affaire Dreyfus*. Paris, 1908.

Cambarieu, A. *Sept ans à l'Elysée*. Paris, 1932.

[de Courcel, Alphonse]. "France et Angleterre en 1895: Lettres de A. de Courcel." *Revue historique*, CCXII (1954), 39–60.

Delcassé, Théophile. *Alerte! Où allons-nous?* Paris, 1882.

Dethan, Georges, ed. "Les Papiers de Gabriel Hanotaux et le proclamation de l'entente franco-russe (1895–1897)." *Revue d'histoire diplomatique*, LXXX (1966), 205–13.

Félix Faure, "Fachoda (1898)." *Revue d'histoire diplomatique*, LXIX (1955), 1–31.

Hanotaux, Gabriel. *Le Partage d'Afrique: Fachoda*. Paris, 1909.

Lebon, André. "La Mission Marchand et le cabinet Méline." *Revue des Deux Mondes*, CLVIII (March 1900), 274–96.

Legrand-Girarde, Général Emile Edmond. *Un Quart de siècle au service de la France, carnets 1894–1918*. Paris, 1954.

Lockroy, Edouard. *La Défense navale*. Paris, 1900. A candid account.

Mangin, C.-M.-E. "Lettres de la mission Marchand, 1895–1899." *Revue des Deux Mondes*, CLXXXIX (September 1931), 241–83.

———. *Regards sur la France d'Afrique*. Paris, 1924.

———. *Souvenirs d'Afrique*. Paris, 1936.

Marchand, Jean-Baptiste. [Account of the Fashoda encounter]. *Le Figaro*, 26 August 1904.

———. [Account of the Fashoda encounter]. *L'Illustration*, 27 January 1934.

———. Statements to *Le Matin*, 20 and 24 June 1905.

———. "Une Lettre inédite de Marchand à Gentil," ed. M.-A. Ménier. *Revue d'histoire des colonies*, XL (1954), 431–40.

———. "Lettres du commandant Marchand à Guillaume Grandidier," ed. M.-A. Ménier. *Revue d'histoire des colonies*, LXV (1958), 61–108.

Maurras, Charles. *Au Signe de flore*. Paris, 1931.

Michel, Charles. *Mission de Bonchamps: vers Fachoda à la rencontre de la mission Marchand*. Paris, 1900.

Monteil, Parfait L. *Souvenirs vécus: quelques feuillets de l'histoire coloniale; les rivalités internationales*. Paris, 1924.

Paléologue, Maurice. *Journal de l'affaire Dreyfus, 1894–1899: l'affaire Dreyfus et le Quai d'Orsay*. Paris, 1956.

Péguy, Charles. "Notes politiques et sociales, l'affaire Dreyfus et la crise du parti socialiste." *Amitié Charles Péguy*, XLVI (1955), 15–22; LIII (1956), 14–28; LIV (1956), 2–18.

Prompt, Victor. "Soudan nilotique." *Bulletin de l'Institut égyptien*, III (1893), 71–116.

b. Britain

Barclay, Thomas. *Thirty Years: Anglo-French Reminiscences*. London, 1914.
Blunt, Wilfrid. *My Diaries*. London, 1932.
Brett, M. V., ed. *Journals and Letters of Reginald, Viscount Esher*, I. London, 1934.
Dawson, Douglas F. (Colonel). *A Soldier-Diplomat*. London, 1927.
Salisbury, Robert, Marquis of. *Essays, 1861–1864, foreign politics*. London, 1905.

PUBLISHED SECONDARY SOURCES

1. FRANCE: THE INTERNAL SETTING

Boussel, P. *L'Affaire Dreyfus et la presse*. Paris, 1960.
Carroll, E. Malcolm. *French Public Opinion and Foreign Affairs, 1870–1914*. New York, 1931.
Chapman, Guy. *The Dreyfus Case: A Reassessment*. London, 1955.
Chastenet, Jacques. *Histoire de la Troisième République, III: La République triomphante, 1893–1906*. Paris, 1955.
Johnson, Douglas. *France and the Dreyfus Affair*. London, 1966. An excellent introduction.
McKay, Donald Vernon. "Colonialism in the French Geographical Movement," *Geographical Review*, XXXIII (1943), 214–32.
Nolte, Ernst. *Three Faces of Fascism: Action Française, Italian Fascism, National Socialism*. New York, 1966.
Peter, Jean-Pierre. "Dimensions de l'affaire Dreyfus." *Annales*, XVI (1961), 1141–67.
Rabaud, Jean. "Pour l'unité socialiste, la première campagne de Jaurès." *Bulletin de la société d'études jaurèsiennes*, III (1962), 1–8.
Reinach, Joseph. *Histoire de l'affaire Dreyfus*, IV. Paris, 1904.
Sorel, Georges. *La Revolution dreyfusienne*. Paris, 1909.
Willard, Claude. *Le Mouvement socialiste en France (1893–1905); les Guesdistes*. Paris, 1965.
Williams, Philip. "Crisis in France: A Political Institution." *Cambridge Journal*, XXXV (October 1963), 36–50.
Winnacker, Rudolph A. "The Influence of the Dreyfus Affair on the Political Development of France." *Papers of the Michigan Academy of Science*, XXX (1936), 465–78.

2. FRANCE: THE EXTERNAL SETTING

Andrew, Christopher. *Théophile Delcassé and the Making of the Entente Cordiale*. New York, 1968.
Balteau, J. et al. *Dictionnaire de biographie française*. Paris, 1933–59.
Baumont, Maurice. "L'Affaire Dreyfus dans la diplomatie française." *Studies in Diplomatic History and Historiography in Honour of G. P. Gooch*, ed. A. O. Sarkissian. London, 1961, pp. 26–47.
———. "L'Affaire Dreyfus et l'opinion italienne d'après les archives diplomatiques." *Rassegna storica del Resorgimento*. IX (1964), 345–50.
———. *Aux Sources de l'affaire; l'affaire Dreyfus d'après les archives diplomatiques*. Paris, 1959.

Berge, François. " Le Sous-Secrétariat et les Sous-Secrétaires d'Etat aux Colonies."
  Revue française d'histoire d'outremer, XLVII (1960), 301–86.
Brunschwig, Henri. *Mythes et réalités de l'impérialisme colonial français, 1871–
  1914*. Paris, 1960.
Cady, John Frank. *The Roots of French Imperialism in Eastern Asia*. New York,
  1954.
Delebecque, Jacques. *Vie du Général Marchand*. Paris, 1936.
Duchêne, A. *La Politique coloniale de la France: le Ministère des Colonies depuis
  Richelieu*. Paris, 1928.
Farmer, Marlin K. " The Foreign Policy of M. Théophile Delcassé." Ph. D. disser-
  tation, Ohio State University, 1937.
Iiams, T. M. *Dreyfus, Diplomatists and the Dual Alliance: Gabriel Hanotaux
  at the Quai d'Orsay (1894–98)*. Paris-Geneva, 1962.
Langer, William L. *The Diplomacy of Imperialism*, 2nd ed. New York, 1951.
Neton, Albéric. *Delcassé*. Paris, 1952.
Newbury, C. W. " The Development of French Policy on the Lower and the
  Upper Niger, 1880–98." *Journal of Modern History*, XXXI (1959), 16–26.
Newbury, C. W., and Kanya-Forstner, A. S. " French Policy and the Origins of the
  Scramble for West Africa." *Journal of African History*, X (1969), 253–76.
Porter, Charles W. *The Career of Théophile Delcassé*. Philadelphia, 1936.
Renouvin, Pierre. *Histoire des relations internationales, VI: Le XIXe siècle*. Paris,
  1955.
————. " L'Orientation de l'alliance franco-russe en 1900–1901." *Revue d'histoire
  diplomatique*, LXXX (1966), 193–204.
————. " Les Origines de l'expédition de Fachoda." *Revue historique*, CC (1948),
  180–97.
————. *La Politique extérieure de Théophile Delcassé 1898–1905*. Paris: Centre
  de Documentation Universitaire, 1954.
————. *La Politique extérieure de la Troisième République de 1871–1904*. Paris:
  Centre de Documentation Universitaire, 1953.
Réquin, Edouard. *Archinard et le Soudan*. Paris, 1945.
Sanderson, G. N. *England, Europe and the Upper Nile, 1882–1899*. Edinburgh,
  1965. This is the best single introduction to both British and French policy.
  It is a mine of information, but at times the narrative becomes so detailed that
  the general themes are lost from view.
Schéfer, Christian. *La Politique coloniale de la monarchie de juillet*. Paris, 1928.
————. " La Politique coloniale de la première restauration: le dessein." *Annales
  des sciences politiques*, XVI (1901), 299–320.
Stengers, Jean. " Aux Origines de Fachoda: l'expédition Monteil." *Revue belge
  de philologie et d'histoire*, XXXVI (1958), 436–50; XXXVIII (1960), 366–
  404, 1040–65.
————. " L'Impérialisme colonial de la fin du XIXe siècle: mythe ou réalité."
  Journal of African History, III (1962), 469–91.
Taboulet, Georges. *Le Geste français en Indochine*. Paris, 1955.
Tramond, Joannes and André Reussner. *Eléments d'histoire maritime et coloniale
  contemporaine (1815–1914)*. Paris, 1924.

3. BRITAIN AND OTHERS

Cecil, Lady G. *Life of Robert, Marquis of Salisbury*, IV. London, 1932.
Collins, R. O. *The Southern Sudan, 1883–1898: A Struggle for Control*. New
  Haven, Conn., 1962.
Frog, John. " L'Affaire Dreyfus vécue en Angleterre." *Libertés françaises*, XVIII
  (1957), 35–46.

Garvin, J. L. *The Life of Joseph Chamberlain.* London, 1934.

Grenville, J. A. S. *Lord Salisbury and Foreign Policy.* London, 1964.

Halperin, Rose A. " The American Reaction to the Dreyfus Affair." Master's thesis, Columbia University, 1941.

Hargreaves, John D. " *Entente Manquée*: Anglo-French Relations, 1895–1896." *Cambridge Historical Journal*, XI (1953), 65–92.

————. " Towards a History of the Partition of Africa." *Journal of African History*, I (1960), 97–109.

Holt, Peter M. *The Mahdist State in the Sudan, 1881–1898.* Oxford, 1958.

————. " The Sudanese Mahdia and the Outside World, 1881–1889." *Bulletin of the School of Oriental and African Studies*, XXI (1958), 276–90.

James, R. R. *Rosebery: A Biography of Archibald Philip, Fifth Earl of Rosebery.* London, 1963.

Marder, A. J. *The Anatomy of British Sea Power: A History of British Naval Policy in the Pre-Dreadnought Era, 1880–1905.* New York, 1940.

Penson, Lillian M. *Foreign Affairs Under the Third Marquess of Salisbury.* London, 1962.

————. " The New Course in British Foreign Policy, 1892–1902." *Transactions of the Royal Historical Society*, Fourth series, XXV (1943), 121–38.

————. " The Principles and Methods of Lord Salisbury's Foreign Policy." *Cambridge Historical Journal*, V (1935), 87–106.

Riker, T. W. " A Survey of British Policy in the Fashoda Crisis." *Political Science Quarterly*, XLIV (1929), 54–78.

Robinson, Ronald, and John Gallagher. *Africa and the Victorians: The Official Mind of Imperialism.* London, 1961.

Sanderson, G. N. " Contributions from African Sources to the History of European Competition in the Upper Valley of the Nile." *Journal of African History*, III (1962), 69–90.

————. " The European Powers and the Sudan in the Later Nineteenth Century." *Sudan Notes and Records*, XL (1959), 79–100.

————. " The Foreign Policy of the Negus Menelik, 1896–1898." *Journal of African History*, V (1964), 87–97.

Taylor, A. J. P. *From Napoleon to Stalin: Comments on European History.* London, 1950.

————. " Prelude to Fashoda: The Question of the Upper Nile, 1894–5." *Economic History Review*, LXV (1950), 52–80.

————. *The Struggle for Mastery in Europe 1848–1918.* Oxford, 1954.

Wood, Leonard C. " Sir Edmund Monson, Ambassador to France." Ph. D. dissertation, University of Pennsylvania, 1960.

4. THEORY AND GENERAL

Barthélemy, Joseph. *Démocratie et politique étrangère.* Paris, 1919.

Braudel, Fernand. " Histoire et sociologie," in Georges Gurvitch *et al.*, *Traité de sociologie*, I, 2nd ed., Paris, 1962, 82–97.

Cairns, John C. " Politics and Foreign Policy: The French Parliament, 1911–1914." *Canadian History Review*, XXXIV (1953), 245–76.

Furniss, Edgar S. *The Office of the Premier in French Foreign Policy-Making: An Application of Decision-making Analysis.* Princeton, 1954.

————. *Weaknesses in French Foreign Policy-Making.* Princeton, 1954.

Leaman, Bertha. " The Influence of Domestic Policy on Foreign Affairs in France, 1898–1905." *Journal of Modern History*, XIV (1942), 449–79.

Mayer, Arno J. *Wilson vs. Lenin, Political Origins of the New Diplomacy, 1917–1918.* Cleveland, 1964.

————. *Politics and Diplomacy of Peacemaking, Containment and Counterrevolution at Versailles, 1918–1919*. New York, 1967.

Meynaud, Jean. *Nouvelles études sur les groupes de pression en France*. Paris, 1962.

Nicolson, Harold. *Diplomacy*, 2nd ed. London, 1950.

Renouvin, Pierre. " L'Histoire contemporaine des relations internationales: orientation de recherches." *Revue historique*, CCXXI (1954), 233–55.

Schéfer, Christian. *D'une Guerre à l'autre. Essai sur la politique extérieure de la Troisième République (1871–1917)*. Paris, 1920.

Schuman, Frederick L. *War and Diplomacy in the Third French Republic*. Chicago, 1931.

Snyder, Richard C., H. W. Bruck, and Burton Sapin. *Foreign Policy Decision-Making: An Approach to the Study of International Politics*. New York, 1962.

Vital, David. "On Approaches to the Study of International Relations." *World Politics*, XIX (1967), 551–63.

Williams, Philip. *Politics in Post-War France*. London, 1958.

INDEX